Nuclear Power

Nuclear Power

Futures, costs and benefits

NIGEL EVANS
and
CHRIS HOPE

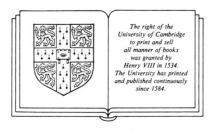

CAMBRIDGE UNIVERSITY PRESS

Cambridge
London   New York   New Rochelle
Melbourne   Sydney

Published by the Press Syndicate of the University of Cambridge
The Pitt Building, Trumpington Street, Cambridge CB2 1RP
32 East 57th Street, New York, NY 10022, USA
296 Beaconsfield Parade, Middle Park, Melbourne 3206, Australia

First published 1984

Printed in Great Britain at The Pitman Press, Bath

Library of Congress catalogue card number: 84–1806

British Library Cataloguing in Publication Data

Evans, Nigel
Nuclear power.
1. Atomic power industry
I. Title   II. Hope, Chris
333.79'24'091821   HD9698.A2

ISBN 0 521 26191 0

PP

To our wives, Christine and Elaine

Contents

Figures

Tables

Abbreviations

AC	alternating current
AECB	Atomic Energy Control Board (of Canada)
AECL	Atomic Energy of Canada Limited
AGR	advanced gas-cooled reactor
AIF	Atomic Industrial Forum
BBC	Brown Boveri Company
B & W	Babcock and Wilcox
BWR	boiling water reactor
CE	Combustion Engineering
CEA	Commissariat à l'Energie Atomique (the French equivalent of the UK Atomic Energy Authority)
CEGB	Central Electricity Generating Board
CHP	combined heat and power
DC	direct current
EDF	Electricité de France (French power utility)
EJ	exa-joule (10^{18} J)
ERL	emergency reference level
FBR	fast breeder reactor
GE	General Electric (US)
GEC	General Electric Company (UK)
GJ	giga-joule (10^9 J)
GPU	General Public Utilities
GW	giga-watt
GWh	giga-watt hour
GWyr	giga-watt year
HTGR	high temperature gas-cooled reactor
IAEA	International Atomic Energy Agency
IEA	International Energy Agency
IIASA	International Institute for Applied Systems Analysis
INFCE	International Nuclear Fuel Cycle Evaluation
JANZ	Japan, Australia, New Zealand
KWU	Kraftwerk Union
LHS	Latin Hypercube Sampling
LP	linear program
LWR	light water reactor
mill	0.001 US $

MIT	Massachusetts Institute of Technology
mtce	million tonnes of coal equivalent
mtoe	million tonnes of oil equivalent
MW	mega-watt
NDB	net decision benefit
NEA	Nuclear Energy Agency
NEC	net effective cost
NII	Nuclear Installations Inspectorate
NODC	non-OPEC developing countries
NPT	Non-Proliferation Treaty
NRC	Nuclear Regulatory Commission
NSSS	nuclear steam supply system
OECD	Organisation for Economic Co-operation and Development
OPEC	Organisation of Petroleum Exporting Countries
PHWR	pressurised heavy water reactor
PJ	peta-joule (10^{15} J)
PRA	probabilistic risk assessment
PRCC	partial rank correlation coefficient
PWR	pressurised water reactor
rem	roentgen equivalent man (dose equivalent unit of radiation; 1 rem = 0.01 Sievert (Sv))
SSEB	South of Scotland Electricity Board
SWU	separative work unit
TJ	tera-joule (10^{12} J)
TMI	Three Mile Island
TMI-1	Three Mile Island – Unit 1 (used to refer to the specific reactor at the TMI site)
TMI-2	Three Mile Island – Unit 2
TWH	tera-watt hour
UCPTE	Union for Cooperation in Production and Transmission of Electricity
UKAEA	United Kingdom Atomic Energy Authority
WASH-1400	Abbreviation used for the first US PRA study, performed in 1975. Also known as the Rasmussen Report.
WOCA	world outside communist areas
WPPSS	Washington Public Power Supply System

Preface

Many books on the subject of nuclear power already exist. Some give a general introduction to the nuclear industry. Others trace the history of policy making in one country or another. Still others, and they form the majority, try to convince the reader that nuclear power is a universal panacea, or that it is an insidious poison. This book does none of these things. Instead, we take the worldwide state of the industry, past policy decisions and current entrenched opinions as our starting point, and look to the future.

In the mid-1970s, in the aftermath of the first oil price shock, nuclear power was widely expected to undergo rapid expansion in most industrialised, and some developing, countries. These expectations have not been realised. We show how doubts about the costs and risks of nuclear power have grown, and how they should be taken into account when making decisions about future options for power generation. These decisions will not generally be made in private by scientists, engineers or economists, but only after extensive public debate and consultation. Our intention in this book is to make our arguments accessible to all who wish to understand this debate, and so our exposition avoids advanced mathematics wherever possible. However, this is not an introductory book. The balance of advantage between nuclear power and its competitors is not clearcut. Decision-making in these circumstances requires the will to follow a tightly reasoned argument. Indeed, the nuclear power debate has become so broad that it would now be impossible to cover all its facets to sufficient depth in a single book. We concentrate here on nuclear power in the world outside Communist areas (WOCA) and, even for the Western world, we do not explicitly address the issues of proliferation, waste disposal, environmental effects (other than their impact on human health), or the purely political aspects of nuclear power. Readers will be able to judge for themselves how easily the methods we propose could be applied to these topics in the future.

For the specialist, we mention that some of the topics appearing here are adapted, with varying degrees of change, from our publications in the academic literature. Chapter 4 is based on a paper by Nigel Evans in *Energy*, 7:9 (1982), pp. 723–30; Chapter 5 on Evans and Hope, *Energy Policy*, 10:4 (1982), pp. 295–304; and Chapter 8 on Evans, *Energy Economics*, 6:1 (1984), pp. 14–20. Large parts of Chapter 6 are based closely on 'Defining risk', a joint paper by Baruch Fischhoff, Stephen Watson and Chris Hope, *Policy Sciences*, (in press). This is the clearest example of our substantial debt to others, but we also express our gratitude to the following who have had considerable influence on the content of this book by their comments, questions and criticisms: Henry Inston and Nick Woollacott of the Programmes and Policy Division of the UK Atomic Energy Authority, numerous staff members of both British Nuclear Fuels Ltd and the Central Electricity Generating Board, and Sir Alan Cottrell and Dr Jeffrey Lewins of Cambridge University. We are also pleased to acknowledge financial support from the Social Science Research Council and Shell International.

To Professor Richard Eden, head of the Cambridge Energy Research Group, we are indebted for far more than the Foreword to this book. We extend our warmest thanks to him and all other staff and students of CERG for many stimulating discussions over the last four years. Production of the final typescript has been supervised by Jan Jenkins, Cynthia Wilcockson and, particularly, Gerie Lonzarich whose skill and patience made 'Just insert this sentence on page 15, would you?' sound like a reasonable request. We thank them all.

NIGEL EVANS
CHRIS HOPE
October 1983

Foreword

by RICHARD EDEN,
Professor of Energy Studies, University of Cambridge

The development of nuclear power is one of the great issues of our time. Thirty years ago it was almost universally accepted as the energy source of the future that would provide cheap electricity for many generations to come, with an environmental impact far more acceptable than fossil fuel. Today, despite an increased awareness of the vulnerability of the world economy to energy scarcity following the two oil crises, nuclear power is at best a difficult option for a government to choose and, at least for the time being, it may not necessarily be the cheapest choice. Proponents may argue the need and safety of nuclear power, but opponents perceive an unacceptable risk of catastrophic accident, or weapons proliferation leading to nuclear war. Values and perceptions of risk differ between proponents and opponents and in Chapter 6 of this book the authors provide an elegant illustration of how these differences affect objectives and conclusions.

Will public attitudes to nuclear power change again – perhaps as dramatically as in the past twenty years? If so, and the view of proponents prove correct, then the proper question is not whether we shall expand nuclear power but when? Even if this view should prevail we can be sure that there will be wide differences between countries, just as past changes in plans for a nuclear future have shown extreme variations from one country to another. These changed views and expectations are reflected by the range of forecasts described in Chapter 2, and the divergence of national policies is underlined in the discussion of nuclear prospects, country by country. The authors do not include the USSR, Eastern Europe and China in their discussion, but it may be relevant to the debate that these countries maintain plans and programmes for nuclear power that appear, so far, to be unaffected by the changed attitudes that are prevalent in much of the non-Communist world.

However, some features of nuclear power are common to many

countries and an accident anywhere in the world may affect attitudes elsewhere. In Chapter 4 the authors examine the worldwide consequences of the accident in the USA in 1979 at the Three Mile Island Unit 2 Pressurised Water Reactor. They show that similar types of reactor elsewhere were operated at lower load factors following the accident, and in Chapter 5 they discuss possible influences of this knock-on effect on estimation of the costs of future reactors – an effect that would be additional to the costs of extra safety measures incorporated in new designs. It is reasonable to suppose that the lower load factors following the accident at Three Mile Island were mainly due to a precautionary response by plant engineers and management rather than a political response to public concern, but decisions on future reactors, or those under construction, may be more directly influenced by public concern. In that accident, no lives were lost, but the public were dramatically reminded of the possibility of reactor core meltdown involving a massive release of radiation and serious injuries and loss of life. In Chapter 3 the authors contrast the results of engineering analysis of probabilities for serious nuclear accidents with the statistical evidence from operating experience on core meltdown, and on meltdown 'precursors'. As operating experience increases it will not only provide more evidence on accident probabilities, but also – provided there are no serious accidents involving loss of life – it will increase public familiarity and confidence in nuclear power.

The response by government and industry to public concern about nuclear power has differed widely from one country to another, influenced partly by the cost of alternatives such as low-cost coal in Australia and in some parts of the USA, but more generally by differing institutional structures – political, legal and social. These have a major effect, not only on public attitudes and political choice, but also on the costs of nuclear power and uncertainties about the costs of new ventures. The problem of incorporating such uncertainties into decision indicators on the economics of nuclear power compared with alternative means of electricity generation is examined in Chapters 7 and 8. The authors' original contributions to this important topic will provide a valuable aid to that part of policy on nuclear power that relates to its comparative economics, rather than to issues of safety and public acceptability.

The wide variations between countries in the costs of nuclear power due to institutional and social differences, including labour practices and skills, will impact on the costs of electricity. At the margin this will lead to increased trade in electricity across national boundaries, which is discussed by the authors in Chapter 9. In the long run the choice of nuclear power for electricity generation and the consequential costs, coupled with the costs in each country of other forms of electricity generation, will have a major impact on industrial structure. Initially it will affect those industries whose use of electricity is high in relation to their output, but later the cost of electricity to all users will influence society as a whole and will change the character of product demand.

The impact of national policies on electricity generation, and on the costs of nuclear power, will be enhanced by an increasing worldwide scarcity of fossil fuel, particularly oil. The changing character and costs of electricity generation, differing from country to country, will change comparative advantages in international trade and affect economic growth. Policies on nuclear power will be an important factor in these changes – their influence is likely to extend far beyond those countries or communities where current decisions are made. In this book the authors have prudently confined their subject matter to more limited questions, where their thoughtful contributions are likely to increase public and professional understanding of different viewpoints. This will not lead to a consensus between proponents and opponents of nuclear power but it may help to clarify the conflict, and it should assist those whose views fall between the extremes but are concerned with the welfare of future generations.

Most of the material presented in this book was developed by the authors as part of their research activity with the Cambridge Energy Research Group (CERG) in the Cavendish Laboratory of the University of Cambridge. This is an interdisciplinary group of faculty, research associates, graduate students, and senior visitors, concerned with a wide variety of topics in energy studies, ranging from the use of energy in industry to aspects of international energy. Dr Nigel Evans joined the group in 1979 after two years experience as a reactor physicist at the Wylfa nuclear power station in Wales. His analysis of world nuclear power prospects, reported in Chapter 2, was a component of a study by CERG of the world energy outlook, and other chapters have their origin in his development of an electricity system model for these international studies. Dr Chris Hope joined CERG from the Department of Energy's Energy Technology Support Unit and completed his Ph.D. in 1979 on methods for assessing investment on research and development for re-newable energy technologies. Subsequently as a post-doctoral research associate in the group he extended the techniques of decision analysis under uncertainty that were used in his thesis and applied them to a range of topics, including collaborative work with Dr Evans on aspects of nuclear power which forms the basis for some chapters in this book.

Dr Hope left the group in January 1983 to become a lecturer in the Department of Fuel and Energy in the University of Leeds.

In this book Nigel Evans and Chris Hope have provided a thoughtful and interesting study of some important issues concerning the future of nuclear power. It should be of value to all those concerned with nuclear futures in the world energy scene.

1

Nuclear power certainties and doubts

Opposition to nuclear power is not new. The earliest attack that we have found dates from 1923.[1] However, in the early years of civilian power generation, in the late 1950s and 1960s, the nuclear industry progressed apparently without difficulty. Programmes of power station construction were initiated in several industrial countries, and plans were made for the rapid introduction of this new source of energy. Any debate and dissent was essentially private, within the confines of the nuclear establishment.

It was not until the 1970s that the opponents of nuclear power began to delay the development of the industry, and the debate entered its public phase. By skilful presentation of the undesirable aspects of nuclear power, objectors won the hearts of many members of the public to the anti-nuclear cause. Members of the nuclear establishment were exasperated that the influence exerted by some nuclear opponents was out of all proportion to the quality of their arguments, which were felt to be technically weak. The degree of unease can be judged from the professional response to the anti-nuclear arguments that began to appear in print.[2]

This response sought to prove that nuclear power was both cheap and safe. Its ultimate conclusion was that no other energy source could meet the ever-increasing demand forecasts implied by plans for worldwide economic growth. Large programmes of nuclear power station construction were therefore inevitable. The professional response appeared to have completely vindicated nuclear power.

This optimism has not been borne out by events. Since the late 1970s, the fortunes of nuclear power have been on the decline. Stations already under construction have been cancelled and plans for future investment have been curtailed. Evidence has accumulated that neither the economic nor the safety case is as clearcut as was indicated by the professional response.

In this chapter we review in more detail the early halcyon days of

1

nuclear power, the inroads made by nuclear opponents, the professional response, and the recent problems.[3]

Halcyon days

The initial development of civilian nuclear power occurred during the period of reconstruction following the Second World War. The advanced technology required was a challenge undertaken in a spirit of optimism. The successful harnessing of such a technically demanding energy source inspired national pride. This achievement led some to forecast a future in which power would be so cheap that it would not be worth the effort of metering. Although early reactors were too expensive to warrant large-scale programmes, the advent of the light water reactor (LWR) in the early 1960s gave the promise of a cost breakthrough. Early LWR stations were supplied on a turnkey basis at prices that undercut the cost of generating electricity from coal. These reactor designs still form the basis of nuclear stations under construction today.

The safety of nuclear power was not an issue. Even such a potentially serious accident as the Windscale fire in 1957 had no impact on nuclear development programmes.[4] The link between nuclear power and weapons, much stronger then than today, was seen as an asset rather than a liability, as the military connection ensured a substantial subsidy for electricity generation. This comfortable certainty continued throughout the 1950s and 1960s, with nuclear power decisions being made in private and with little input from outside the nuclear industry.

Opposition inroads

In the 1970s the debate went public, and nuclear opponents were able to affect substantially the progress of the nuclear industry. In the USA this was achieved primarily by a skilful exploitation of the existing machinery for public consultation. Doubts were cast upon the safety of nuclear plants in routine operation, and concerns over catastrophic accidents were emphasised. 'The possibilities of delay were brilliantly exploited by the environmentalist groups, who rose to a new peak of influence.'[5] In some European countries nuclear opposition took the form of mass public demonstrations. All this led to widespread frustration inside the nuclear industry. There was general agreement that the evidence presented by opponents was sketchy and incomplete. The objectors claimed this was an inevitable result of their limited resources; nuclear proponents were not convinced. They prepared a closely reasoned defence of nuclear power with the aim of publicly discrediting the claims of the opposition once and for all.

The professional response

We summarise the response of the nuclear industry in the following paragraphs.[6] The language reflects the certainty felt by nuclear proponents that their case was logically watertight. It should not be taken as an indication that this case still appears correct to us now.

The need for energy

The great increases in wealth that had been achieved by most nations over the last few decades had been accompanied by a corresponding growth in the demand for energy. The strong correlation between the use of energy and the creation of wealth had a very general validity and was applicable to countries with widely differing per capita incomes. If we wished to enjoy continued improvements in our standard of living then we had to ensure a similar increase in the supply of energy. Conservation could go some way towards alleviating this need in the most advanced nations with capital to spare, but even here its impact would not be great. For the Third World there would be no alternative to a rapidly increasing use of energy if their economies were to grow at anything like the rate needed to abolish the appalling poverty that still existed in many places. Thus selfishness and altruism both pointed to the need to increase the available supply of energy as a matter of priority.

Coal and nuclear were the only viable options for long-term energy supply. The end of the road was in sight for oil, as the large price increases of the early 1970s had indicated. Even if exhaustion were not imminent, continued reliance on the volatile Middle East for a large fraction of our energy supply would have been unwise. Potential supplies of oil from non-OPEC sources were much smaller and would take many years to develop.

Natural gas production would shortly begin to decline in its major historical market, the United States. Potential suppliers for the future lay in the Middle East or the Communist bloc, not ideal partners politically for prospective Western customers. Natural gas was neither as cheap nor as safe as oil to transport over long distances.

Hydroelectricity was locally important in many countries, but in most industrial nations nearly all the best sites had already been exploited, so a greatly increased contribution from hydropower could not take place. Other renewable energy sources such as solar-, wind- and wavepower showed promise for the long term but all required lengthy development programmes before they could be brought into use with any degree of confidence. As for fusion, not even the basic principles of power generation had yet been demonstrated.

Therefore the choice for the future lay between an increasing nuclear power programme and a re-emergence of coal to its dominant position of the late nineteenth century. There was no imminent physical shortage either of coal or of nuclear fuel. Economics and safety were the only criteria against which the two options were to be judged.

Economics

The oil price rises of 1973 made oil-fired generation uneconomic, and the price of coal rose in response. Baseload nuclear power enjoyed a definite economic advantage, ranging from 10 to 60%, depending on the location and the accounting conventions used to add together capital and running costs. This advantage would continue or even increase. Coal would be required in future to replace oil and gas in many uses, either directly or after conversion to a more convenient gaseous or liquid fuel. This would inevitably require a large increase in international coal trade leading to rising costs and prices to restore equilibrium in the market.[7] A great many of the assumptions incorporated in these economic studies were subject to some uncertainty, but the size of the projected cost advantage meant that nuclear could only turn out to be uneconomic if the majority of them proved to be quite badly wrong.

Safety

The impact of nuclear power on the environment during normal operation would be small, since the quantities of fuel required per unit of electricity output were so much less than for fossil-fuelled generation. The operation of nuclear power stations would be so tightly monitored that any radiation hazard to the public would normally be negligible, and certainly far less than the natural background radiation. Disposal of radioactive waste would be cheap and easy, again largely because of the small quantities involved. The only reason that a method of permanent disposal had not yet been perfected was that it was not yet needed. The possibility of material from civil reactors being diverted for military uses did exist, but the appropriate political response was through the nuclear non-proliferation treaty. Cutting back civil nuclear power programmes would have no effect on countries determined to create nuclear weapons, since the raw materials for these could be supplied with great ease from specially built small-scale plutonium-producing plants. Indeed, cutbacks in nuclear electricity generation might have increased the likelihood of nuclear war by intensifying the competition for the remaining sources of fossil fuels.

This left the large power station accident as the final risk to public safety from nuclear electricity generation. This risk was addressed by an exhaustive study, published in 1975, by the Nuclear Regulatory Commission (NRC), the nuclear industry's independent watch-dog in the USA. This report is commonly referred to either by its report number, WASH-1400, or as the Rasmussen report, after its principal author, Professor Norman Rasmussen of MIT.[8] Rasmussen concluded that there was only about one chance in three million per year that an accident at a nuclear plant would cause ten or more deaths.[9] As with the economic case there were uncertainties surrounding this number, but the very smallness of this risk allowed a considerable margin for error in the calculations before the hazard even approached the dangers that were a familiar consequence of generating electricity from coal.

The final step in the analysis was taken in a study performed for the Atomic Energy Control Board of Canada (AECB) in 1978.[10] This study considered all possible sources of risk from power plants, not just in operation, but also in construction, fuel supply, maintenance and decommissioning. Nuclear power turned out to be between one and two orders of magnitude safer than coal. This much was expected. What surprised many observers was that the study concluded that nuclear power was also more than an order of magnitude less harmful than the renewable sources of electricity, which were traditionally felt to be benign. The low energy densities available to the renewables meant large inputs of materials, labour and maintenance for each unit of electricity generated, which together gave a significant total risk. This was the final confirmation of the safety of nuclear power. It was not only less risky than coal, but also safer than the renewable sources which were being advocated, often by those worried about the dangers of nuclear power.

The nuclear camp had all the answers. Nuclear power was necessary, cheap and safe. The logic behind this case appeared irrefutable to many informed observers. They felt that anyone who continued to oppose the rapid buildup of nuclear power programmes worldwide had to be either ill-informed or pursuing devious political ends.[11] In either case their objections could be ignored and the pace of nuclear development maintained. Figure 1.1 shows some of the forecasts of future nuclear capacity that were made around this time. The upward-thrusting lines show the consensus professional view in the mid-1970s of the future of nuclear power.[12]

Recent problems

Since the professional response was made public, the nuclear industry has

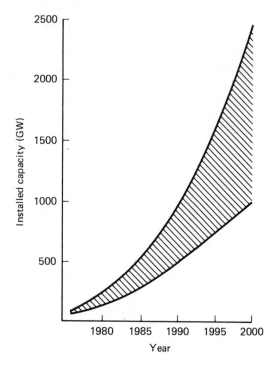

Figure 1.1 Mid-1970s forecasts of nuclear power growth in the world outside Communist areas

exhibited more signs of decline than of dramatic advance. For example, in the USA there have been just two new orders for nuclear stations since 1977. Compare this with 18 nuclear projects cancelled in 1982 alone. Far from being discredited by the professional response, doubts about the economics and safety of nuclear power have been more thoroughly documented in the recent past than ever before.

Initially, only the odd dissenting voice asserted that coal-fired electricity generation was cheaper than nuclear, even in countries with high cost coal such as the UK.[13] But by the early 1980s it was becoming apparent that the capital costs of nuclear stations were increasing rapidly, even after allowing for the effects of general inflation.[14] These increases were something like 15% per year between commissioning years of 1973 and 1979, for Westinghouse Stations in the USA. Forward projections of cost escalation for reactors under construction indicated that the real cost increase would continue at about 10% per year at least until the mid-1980s.[15] Some of the mid-1970s studies that had initially shown a cost advantage to nuclear were re-analysed, substituting actual construction and operating performance for the original estimates. The adjusted lifetime costs now favoured coal.[16] Economic growth rates were falling everywhere and forecasts of required generating capacity were dropping with them.

Even the safety case was tarnished. In 1979 the NRC issued a policy statement that could only be interpreted as a rejection of the methods and results of the Rasmussen report.[17] The AECB study claiming the renewables to be more risky than nuclear power stirred up a hornet's nest of technical criticism of its methods and conclusions.[18] And the worst nuclear accident to date occurred at the Three Mile Island unit-2 reactor in Pennsylvania. This incident caused widespread alarm and sent nuclear regulators back to their drawing boards for a lengthy re-evaluation of safety criteria that is still continuing.

Nuclear power has been afflicted by a creeping paralysis. In the next chapter we construct, in some detail, worldwide forecasts of nuclear capacity that look reasonable to us now. It will probably come as no surprise to the majority of readers that our projections lie well below the ranges shown in figure 1.1. There is little scope for them to be proved pessimistic, since stations that are presently being approved or are under construction set the limit to installed capacity for at least the next decade. Even if the paralysis of nuclear power proves to be only a passing affliction, its effects will be felt at least until the 1990s.

Making decisions

Even now governments around the world are still extolling the virtues of nuclear power. There seems to be a reluctance to come to terms with the serious condition of the nuclear industry. This leads to an inability or unwillingness to devise appropriate analytical methods that acknowledge the existence of doubts and uncertainties but still allow a decision to be reached. Instead there seems to be a widespread belief that if the old professional responses are repeated for long enough, like some mystical mantra, they will lead the nuclear industry back to a state of renewed vigour. We feel that if more appropriate techniques are not employed, there is a possibility that we shall slip into a no-nuclear future not through choice but by default. We believe such an outcome to be unsatisfactory.

The bulk of this book, Chapters 3 to 9, contains our suggestions for, and applications of, appropriate techniques for nuclear power decision-making. Most of our examples in these later chapters are drawn from the UK but the points they make are international. A question mark hangs over the future of nuclear power. Understanding how to take decisions in the face of this uncertainty is what this book is about.

2

Nuclear power in the Western world to 2000

In this chapter we evaluate the likely future development of nuclear power in the world outside communist areas (WOCA). This evaluation represents the latest in a long line of similar work which has been conducted during the last decade or so, the overriding feature of all the studies being the fall in estimates for future installed nuclear capacity which has occurred since the early 1970s.[1-5] This downturn is quantified in table 2.1 in which estimates of WOCA nuclear capacity in 1985 and 1990 are given. It may be seen that, in 1972, nuclear capacity was estimated to be 1068 GW by 1990; similar estimates produced in this chapter lie in the range 268–331 GW.

Within the general picture of low nuclear growth in WOCA, exceptions emerge. Most notable is the case of France, where nuclear capacity has grown rapidly in a programme which was started as late as 1973. South Korea and Taiwan are examples of developing countries which are pursuing ambitious nuclear programmes as part of their overall economic plans. These countries provide an indication of rates of nuclear expansion which are possible given a favourable combination of political commitment and external pressures (e.g. lack of indigenous energy sources) and point to the need for some caution before forecasting capacity figures for the long term which fall well below the lower bounds of previous estimates.

Methodology

The methodology employed in this chapter is similar to that adopted in a recent OECD/NEA evaluation.[6] We make no attempt to model formally the expansion of nuclear power in the Western world, as has been done in some studies,[7] because we feel that future levels of nuclear capacity depend strongly on a large number of local factors within a country, and cannot be evaluated simply from a regional energy supply/demand

9

Table 2.1 *The evolving pattern of nuclear capacity projections (GW)*

	Data source	Year of projection	1985		1990	
North America						
	(1)	1972	295		539	
	(2)	1975	223		426	
	(3)	1977	125–157		214–	287
	(4)	1979	112–134		177–	214
	(5)	1980	96–119		138–	156
	this book	1983	84–105		113–	135
Western Europe						
	(1)	1972	184		373	
	(2)	1975	165–212		264–	380
	(3)	1977	107–146		195–	273
	(4)	1979	100–113		166–	209
	(5)	1980	94– 95		142–	157
	this book	1983	81– 95		109–	127
OECD Pacific						
	(1)	1972	63		106	
	(2)	1975	49		85	
	(3)	1977	27– 40		50–	80
	(4)	1979	26– 33		45–	60
	(5)	1980	28– 30		51–	53
	this book	1983	20– 23		27–	33
Developing World						
	(1)	1972	25		50	
	(2)	1975	46		114	
	(3)	1977	19– 25		45–	60
	(4)	1979	19– 23		45–	50
	(5)	1980	14		30–	33
	this book	1983	10– 15		19–	23
WOCA						
	(1)	1972	567		1068	
	(2)	1975	479–530		875–1004	
	(3)	1977	278–368		504–	700
	(4)	1979	257–303		434–	534
	(5)	1980	232–258		361–	399
	this book	1983	194–238		268–	331

Note: Sources (1)–(5) are documented in notes 1–5.

analysis. For this reason we consider each country in turn, not by relying on official government plans, which have consistently been over-optimistic in the past, but by focussing attention on a number of local parameters which we consider to be of importance. The parameters which we explicitly consider are:

- Current total installed generating capacity
- Past growth rates of installed capacity
- Past growth rates of electricity demand
- Current installed nuclear generating capacity
- Indigenous energy reserves, particuarly coal and hydro
- Official plans for additional nuclear plants
- Public and political attitudes to nuclear power
- Level of nuclear expertise available locally.

We give the installed nuclear capacity in 1978 and 1982 and also provide estimates for 1985, 1990 and 2000 (all figures refer to the end of the year in question). These estimates are obtained, via the parameters above, by employing judgement to produce a plausible range of capacity figures for each of the future spot years. Uncertainty increases with the time horizon considered in such a way that capacity estimates to 1985 and even 1990 are reasonably well determined (as dictated by the long lead-time for nuclear projects, typically of the order of ten years), while estimates for the end of the century, of necessity, often cover a wider range.

No attempt is made to provide nuclear capacity estimates beyond the year 2000. Such a long-term view is clearly important, but the purpose of this chapter is to illustrate how changes in perceptions regarding nuclear power have had an impact which will be felt to the end of the century. Beyond the year 2000 the uncertainty regarding the energy scene in general, and nuclear power in particular, is such that estimates of ranges of nuclear capacity in 2025, say, would be very broad and few conclusions relevant to the current slowdown in nuclear growth could be drawn. In addition, by restricting our time horizon to the end of the century, we are implicitly confining our discussion to the development of thermal nuclear power, principally in the form of LWR technology. Although some fast reactors will be operational, their numbers will be small and they will be confined to a limited number of countries.[8]

We argue in Chapter 5 that, for any future year, the lower bound on nuclear capacity for all countries is zero, reflecting a worldwide response to some severe nuclear accident. We do not consider this possibility here, but, for countries which currently have a moratorium on nuclear power development, we do adopt lower bounds of zero for future nuclear capacity, to reflect current misgivings regarding the technology.

We give ranges for future capacity such that there is approximately an

80% probability that the actual outcome will be within the range specified. In most cases, the distribution is asymmetric, with capacity figures nearer the lower end of the range being more likely. For this reason, we do not recommend the use of figures mid-way between the specified upper and lower bounds as a representation of the most likely outcome. In some instances we give single capacity figures in preference to ranges, reflecting the view that any other outcome is considered unlikely.

To facilitate comparison between the analysis of this chapter and other studies (as has been done in table 2.1), it is necessary to aggregate individual country data into regional and, ultimately, WOCA figures. Here a problem arises in determining how lower and upper capacity figures for individual countries should be combined to produce lower and upper regional figures. If there is zero correlation between future rates of nuclear construction in different countries, it would be incorrect to sum all low country figures to produce a regional low figure for a given year. However, if there is perfect correlation between nuclear development across all countries, summing all the low figures would be the correct procedure to follow. The actual situation lies between these extremes. For example, if the current economic recession in Western countries is longer and deeper than most observers are currently predicting, it is likely that electricity demand in all OECD countries will fall below current expectations and that future nuclear requirements in all countries will tend towards the lower end of the range of capacity figures given. On the other hand, even within this scenario, the response of a country with a major commitment to nuclear power is likely to be much different from one which currently has moved no further than the initial planning stage.

In this chapter we resolve the above dilemma by simply adding low figures for individual countries to produce a regional low, and likewise for high capacity figures. This is in line with the approach used in the studies referred to in table 2.1. Given the asymmetric nature of the distribution of future installed capacity figures discussed above, it is likely that regional low figures will represent a reasonable low capacity figure whereas the high regional figures very much represent an upper bound, there being significantly less than a 10% probability of exceeding these figures.

The results of this analysis appear in table 2.2, with individual country surveys following in the next section, arranged under regional headings. A large number of data sources have been used in compiling the country profiles. In addition to references which were of relevance to specific countries, certain publications were found to be generally useful.[9]

Unless stated otherwise, nuclear capacity figures are expressed as net giga-watts of electricity output (henceforth written as GW where

Table 2.2 *Net installed nuclear capacity (GW), by country*

	1978	1982	1985 Low	1985 High	1990 Low	1990 High	2000 Low	2000 High
Canada	5.5	7.0	9.0	10.1	11.6	13.3	18	23
USA	55	63	75	95	101	135	130	180
Austria	0	0	0	0	0	0	0	0.7
Belgium	1.7	3.5	4.5	5.5	5.5	5.5	5.5	8
Finland	0.4	2.2	2.2	2.2	2.2	2.2	3	4
France	4.6	23.3	35	40	50	56	70	90
Germany	5.6	9.8	12.6	16	19	23	28	40
Italy	1.4	1.3	1.3	1.3	2	3	7	12
Netherlands	0.5	0.5	0.5	0.5	0.5	0.5	0	3
Spain	1	2	5	7.5	7.5	11.5	12.5	20
Sweden	3.7	7.4	7.4	9.5	9.5	9.5	7	12
Switzerland	1	2	3	3	3	4	4	5
UK	5.8	5.8	9	9	10	11.5	10	17
Other Western Europe	0	0	0	0	0	0	3	10
Japan	11	17	20	23	27	33	60	95
Aust. & NZ	0	0	0	0	0	0	0	2
OPEC	0	0	0	0	0	0	0	2
Argentina	0.4	0.4	1.0	1.0	1.7	1.7	2.7	3.7
Brazil	0	0.6	0.6	0.6	2	3	4.5	7
Egypt	0	0	0	0	0	0	2	5
India	0.6	0.8	1.3	1.5	1.7	2.6	7	10
Korea	0.6	0.6	1.8	3.6	5.4	7.2	11	18
Mexico	0	0	0	1.3	1.3	1.3	3	7
Philippines	0	0	0	0.6	0.6	0.6	0.6	1.2
South Africa	0	0	1.8	1.8	1.8	1.8	3	6
Taiwan	0.6	3.1	3.1	4.9	4.9	4.9	7.5	14
Other NODCs	0	0	0	0	0	0	2	7
Total WOCA	99	150	194	238	268	331	401	603

1 GW = 1000 MW) and, where no decimal point is indicated, are rounded to the nearest GW.

North America

Canada

The total independence in the field of commercial nuclear power that has characterised Canadian interests in this area since the Second World War has in some ways been similar to the UK approach. However, the experience in the UK over the past twenty years appears to illustrate the many disadvantages of such a strategy, whereas Canadian experience points to the advantages of developing a completely independent reactor system.

The Canadian Candu reactor system uses heavy water coolant and moderator and natural uranium fuel. Development of the system has been extremely successful and the performance of the two 4-unit stations at Pickering and Bruce has been among the best of any nuclear stations in the world. Until recently, these two stations represented the full extent of commercial nuclear power in Canada. (The two smaller Douglas Point and Gentilly 1 reactors, totalling 456 MW of capacity, are essentially development prototypes of the Candu system with fairly poor operational histories. By the end of 1982 Gentilly 1 had been non-operational for several years and further power generation from this plant is unlikely.) However, significant additional nuclear expansion is currently underway with single reactors recently coming into service at Gentilly (unit 2) and Point Lepreau and four reactors at each of the major sites of Pickering and Bruce nearing completion. (Pickering 5 received an operating licence towards the end of 1982.) Development at a further site, Darlington, with four more reactors in the planning phase or early stages of construction, is also in progress. However, reduced electricity demand forecasts have resulted in revised construction schedules at this site with the last of the four units now not due to be commissioned until 1992.

The development of Canadian nuclear power has been characterised by continuing cautious progress, with successive increases in unit size being rather modest. The Pickering reactors are 515 MW (net) units, those at Bruce 740 MW and the latest Darlington reactors are of 818 MW capacity. There are no plans at present to move to large 1300 MW units as has been the case in France, USA and West Germany, although Atomic Energy of Canada Limited (AECL), the state-owned concern responsible for the development of the Candu system, has recently produced a conceptual design for a 950 MW reactor which it is hoped will be able to compete successfully in international markets. In addition, the delays and cost overruns which have been experienced in the Canadian nuclear programme have generally not been anything like as severe as those witnessed in countries such as the USA and UK.

Opposition to nuclear power in Canada has been much less strong than in West Germany and the USA although some opposition in Quebec has been experienced recently during construction of the Gentilly 2 reactor. There are probably two major reasons why severe problems of public acceptability have not been encountered. Firstly, the fact that Canada has no nuclear weapons capability means that opposition groups do not associate civil and military uses to the same extent as in some other countries and, secondly, the Candu's record of consistently good performances serves as an effective counter to opponents' misgivings. It should perhaps be noted that the high capital cost of Candu reactors (compared with pressurised water reactors (PWRs), for example) means that high load factors are essential if the system is to be economically viable.

The total generating capacity in Canada in 1980 was in the region of 80 GW, with 45 GW being hydro. Approximately 4% of electricity is generated by oil-fired plant. Nuclear capacity to 1990 is well defined, the only significant uncertainty being in the possible delay of the first two Darlington reactors which are scheduled for completion in mid-1988 and early 1989.

Beyond 1990 nuclear growth is likely to be modest. There is still significant hydro potential in some areas, and the rapid growth in total electricity capacity in recent years means there will be little plant retirement before the end of the century so plant replacement will not be significant. Further nuclear expansion is possible in Ontario and additional development of the Point Lepreau site in New Brunswick (with some of the capacity being committed to US markets) should not be ruled out. Quebec is also a possibility for nuclear development as many of the hydro sites still available in the province may only be exploited at very high cost. With the completion of the Darlington reactors, 15 GW of nuclear capacity will be installed by 1992 or a little later. We estimate that the capacity by the end of the century will be in the range of 18–23 GW.

Canada nuclear capacity (GW)	
1978	5.5
1982	7.0
1985	9.0–10.1
1990	11.6–13.3
2000	18–23

It must be emphasised that most of the pressures for increasing nuclear capacity will not arise because of high electricity demand growth and the threat of capacity shortages, but instead will come from the Canadian nuclear industry, concerned that a low level of ordering will result in the demise of the Candu system. Some success in winning export orders has been achieved and Candus are in operation or under construction in Argentina, South Korea and India with Romania likely to follow suit. However, the immediate prospects for Candu exports are bleak, and AECL have been forced to lay off large numbers of staff. This is in spite of

the fact that the reactor has many supporters worldwide.[10] By main-
taining a steady rate of ordering at home, the survival of the Canadian
nuclear industry may be assured, particularly as this would serve as a
'shop window' for future sales abroad in a world market which may
appear more buoyant in the 1990s.

USA

The late 1960s and early 1970s saw a rapid growth in the
development of nuclear power in the US. By 1976, however, a dramatic
decline in the fortunes of the nuclear industry was taking place due to
factors such as the downturn in growth of electricity demand, significant
time and cost overruns, and increases in regulatory requirements, which
frequently necessitated costly retro-fitting. This decline, which was
already well established by March 1979, was exacerbated by the Three
Mile Island (TMI) accident. During the period 1970–5 orders were placed
for 144 new commercial power reactors. Since 1977 there have been just
two new orders placed (both prior to TMI), and a large number of projects
have been cancelled (eighteen in 1982 alone).

In addition, there is significant public opposition to nuclear power in
the US. The anti-nuclear movement is well organised and articulate with
young middle-class Americans contributing significantly to its ranks. Full
use is made of the US legal system to obtain delays in licensing planned
stations and to defer power-raising at reactors where construction has
been completed. (This is in marked contrast to the limited use made of the
courts by nuclear opponents in the UK.) The rigorous policing of the
nuclear industry by the Nuclear Regulatory Commission (NRC) further
contributes to delays at all stages from planning to full power operation.

The US nuclear industry is dominated by two nuclear steam supply
system (NSSS) manufacturers. Westinghouse produce the PWR and General Electric (GE) the boiling water reactor (BWR). Both have enjoyed
considerable success in transferring reactor technology abroad either by
supplying stations on a turnkey basis (a method favoured in the early days
of nuclear trade), by building reactors in conjunction with local industries, or by granting licences for construction to foreign companies. (The
most striking example here is the case of the French company Framatome
which acquired a PWR licence from Westinghouse in 1958.)

Two other US companies also have PWR capabilities, Combustion
Engineering (CE) and Babcock and Wilcox (B & W). Given the generally
weak state of the US nuclear industry, it is unlikely that all four reactor
vendors will be able to maintain their positions in the market. B & W, as
suppliers of the NSSS at TMI, have already been effectively ruled out of
further sales, and there is evidence that GE are diversifying away from the

supply of complete nuclear units. It now appears that Westinghouse will emerge from the 1980s as the dominant US supplier.[11]

Total installed generating capacity in the US in 1980 was 631 GW of which 56.5 GW was nuclear. In the same year, electricity generation was provided as follows: coal 52%, gas 14%, hydro 12%, oil 11% and nuclear 11%. By the end of 1982, installed nuclear capacity had risen to 63 GW (excluding military and research reactors and the ill-fated TMI-2), and for the first time nuclear units generated more electricity than oil-fired plant in a single year.

Two problems arise when trying to obtain capacity figures to 1990 from data on power stations under construction. Firstly, the extremely long delays currently being experienced in the construction of reactors means that planned completion dates may not be met. Secondly, the current US trend of cancelling not only reactors which have reached the planning stage, but also certain reactors on which construction is well advanced, means that even mid-term future capacity estimates could be significantly below reasonable expectations. For this reason it is prudent to consider future plans, as outlined by plant construction schedules, to represent upper bounds for nuclear capacity, at least until 1990.

For example, a recent Atomic Industrial Forum (AIF) estimate[12] puts nuclear capacity by the end of 1985 at around 95 GW. We assume that this represents an upper bound (even this figure requires that 29 units be brought on-line in the three years 1983–5), and adopt capacity figures in the range 75–95 GW for 1985.

Approximately 147 GW of nuclear capacity is planned to be in operation by 1990, a figure which, in practice, is unlikely to be attained. We adopt a lower value for 1990 of 101 GW, which is slightly below the forecast 1986 level, and assume that 135 GW represents a reasonable upper bound.

Beyond 1990 the picture is even more uncertain. Electricity demand in the period 1990–2000 is projected to grow at around 2.5% per annum. If capacity expansion approximately follows this growth rate and the majority of new stations are nuclear or coal (with a small amount of further exploitation of hydro), nuclear capacity by the year 2000 would be in the region of 500 GW, taking account of the replacement of oil power stations which will inevitably be required during this period. In practice this figure is unrealistic. If there were to be even a slight possibility of capacity increasing from around 120 GW in 1990 to 500 GW in 2000 we would have to be witnessing a huge upturn in nuclear ordering now, in the early 1980s. Because such an upturn is not being experienced, indeed cancellations and deferrals continue apace, we adopt a maximum figure of 180 GW for the installed nuclear capacity in the year 2000. Even this figure would require some upturn in nuclear ordering within the next five years. Our lower figure of 130 GW represents a situation in which project cancellations continue, and no new orders are forthcoming within a timescale which would enable further plant to be commissioned by the end of the century.

An important point emerges from the above estimates. If nuclear capacity is restricted to the ranges of figures indicated, either capacity expansion will be met by other types of plant, or demand growth will fall below the assumed rates. In the short term the proportion of electricity generation met by gas-fired plant is likely to increase but this will be almost exclusively at the expense of oil. For utilities which have cancelled major nuclear projects, the choice is either to embark on no new plant construction (reflecting the fact that current estimates of future demand are much lower than those of the recent past) or to build coal-fired plant, possibly of capacity less than that originally planned for the nuclear unit. For example, Long Island Lighting Co. is now investigating the ramifications of building an 800 MW coal-fired plant to replace the loss of potential supply when the 2300 MW Jamesport nuclear project was scrapped.

The overall outcome of the present situation is likely, in the near term, to be a higher proportion of generation met by coal, gas and even oil than other estimates have suggested, with a further possibility that demand growth will become supply limited in the mid-to-late 1990s. Such a restriction would inevitably lead to an upturn in both nuclear and coal plant construction.

Within this generally pessimistic picture of nuclear development in the US, cases of reasonable progress occasionally emerge. For example, construction of the three Palo Verde reactors in Arizona has proceeded with few delays and has benefited greatly from replication of units. As a contrast, the Washington Public Power Supply System (WPPSS) reactors in Washington state and Diablo Canyon reactors in California, are case studies on how not to build nuclear reactors. Of the 5-unit reactor programme initiated by WPPSS in the 1970s, two units have been cancelled outright and two have been 'mothballed' (work suspended for a number of years), largely because of capital cost overruns and difficulties with project financing. The most recent plant to be mothballed, unit 3, was, ironically, 60% complete and meeting very stringent production targets when funds finally dried up in May 1983.

The farcical situation encountered in late 1981 at Diablo Canyon in California, site of twin 1100 MW PWRs owned by Pacific Gas and Electric, has had an effect on the credibility of nuclear power in the US second only to that of the TMI accident. As preparations were being made to load fuel into unit 1, thirteen years after construction began, it was noticed that diagrams showing the location of major pipework were incorrect – unit 1 had been built to the unit 2 design and vice-versa! Not surprisingly, the NRC called a halt to proceedings because of concern that other design errors might exist, and suspended the low-power operating licence for unit 2.

For the long-term future, the overall level of confidence in the nuclear industry will depend on whether the large number of reactors still under construction can be completed without further significant delay, and, once completed, whether they can perform reliably and achieve reasonable load factors. Further errors on the same scale as the Diablo Canyon affair will not be tolerated lightly by either the public or regulatory bodies.

US nuclear capacity (GW)	
1978	55
1982	63
1985	75–95
1990	101–135
2000	130–180

Western Europe

Austria

In 1980 the total net installed generating capacity in Austria was around 13 GW with a little under 8 GW being hydro plant. Austria has one nuclear station, the 692 MW BWR at Zwentendorf, near Vienna, for which the German company Kraftwerk Union (KWU) was the main contractor and architect–engineer. However, following a public referendum in November 1978, nuclear power was rejected by the Austrians and start-up of the station was prevented by a law of 15 December 1978. As the station was essentially complete at the time of the referendum, GKT, the utility owning the reactor, have incurred considerable costs with no return and are currently pressing for government compensation.

It is thought in some areas that the Austrian Chancellor may have unwittingly caused this state of affairs by making the issue a political one instead of allowing it to be a straight yes or no vote on nuclear energy. The December 1978 law may only be overturned by a two-thirds majority of parliament and this must then be confirmed by a further referendum.

The rejection of nuclear power (which took place before the TMI accident) should be viewed as one component of the overall Austrian energy picture. At present fuel accounts for approximately 60% of the national import bill. With 60% of hydro potential having been exploited and the future electricity growth rate officially estimated to be of the order of 3% per annum, at least for the next decade, it would appear that Austria will have to depend increasingly on coal imports. There is a real possibility that the government will be faced with severe long-term, energy-related balance-of-payments problems.

There has recently been considerable discussion on the possible start-up of the Zwentendorf reactor. Once again, however, the discussion has been placed firmly in the political arena and the major parties appeared unwilling to support start-up of the reactor for fear of losing the support of the crucial environmental ('green') vote in the national elections of April 1983.

We therefore assume that the Zwentendorf reactor will not be operational by 1990, given the widespread opposition to nuclear power. (Recent opinion polls suggest that 45% of voters would oppose a start-up of the plant in a second referendum.) For the year 2000, 692 MW will represent the maximum installed capacity as we assume that no new nuclear construction will be started during the next ten years, even if there is a change of heart regarding operation of Zwentendorf. Perhaps the greatest uncertainty at present concerns the time for which the Zwentendorf plant may remain mothballed before significant capital expenditure is required for possible future operation.

Austria nuclear capacity (GW)	
1978	0
1982	0
1985	0
1990	0
2000	0–0.7

Belgium

Belgium has no gas or oil and uses little coal, domestic production being limited to about 6 million tonnes/yr. With oil imposing a severe balance-of-payments problem, the country's energy strategy has been aimed at fuel substitution combined with industrial restructuring away from oil. The extent to which this policy has been successful may be seen by noting that the contribution of oil to electricity supply has fallen from 51% in 1973 to 34% in 1980 and is projected to be a mere 9% by 1985.

In 1980 the total installed generating capacity in Belgium was just over 11 GW. Hydro capacity accounted for 1.2 GW, and nuclear around

1.7 GW of the total. Three commercial nuclear reactors have been operational since 1975: two Westinghouse PWRs each of 390 MW capacity at Doel and an 870 MW PWR, supplied by the French company Framatome, at Tihange. The Doel and Tihange sites are being further developed with the construction of a 900 MW French PWR and a 1000 MW Westinghouse reactor at each site. Doel 3 and Tihange 2 (both are French units) came into service towards the end of 1982, and the remaining two reactors are scheduled to be operational by 1983 (Doel 4) and 1985 (Tihange 3). These latest reactors are being constructed with considerable input from Belgian industry.

In addition to the seven reactors in operation or at an advanced stage of construction, utility plans call for the construction of two further reactors, each of 1300 MW capacity, to come on-line between 1991 and 1995. There is also provision to build 2 GW of coal plant in the 1990s if high electricity demand growth is maintained. However, there are a number of reasons for supposing that nuclear capacity in 2000 will be no greater than about 8 GW (the seven committed reactors plus the two possible 1300 MW units). Firstly, the relatively small size of the Belgian grid means that nuclear capacity is likely to represent something in the region of 50% of the total by 2000. Export of electricity to neighbouring countries is a possibility, and the replacement of high-cost oil-fired generation with nuclear will continue. Nevertheless, growth of nuclear capacity at a rate greater than that indicated by current plans could lead to nuclear units having to operate at intermediate load rather than baseload.

A second reason for supposing that the growth of Belgian nuclear capacity post-1990 will not continue apace, lies in the opportunity for import of nuclear electricity from France. Considerable cooperation between the two countries already exists, with output from the French station at Chooz and the first Tihange reactor in Belgium being shared equally. There is a strong possibility of Belgian support for future development with the French of the site at Chooz, and the large nuclear site at Gravelines in northern France (ultimate capacity 6×920 MW) is also conveniently situated for electricity export to Belgium. The exact extent to which Franco–Belgian cooperation is developed depends on the rate of growth of electricity demand in France and the capacity utilisation of the French nuclear plant suppliers, as discussed in Chapter 9.

Belgium therefore emerges as a country with limited indigenous energy resources which is committed to nuclear power but which is likely to pursue further development cautiously and at a modest rate. A recently concluded parliamentary debate on the country's energy future has called for the construction of a 600 MW coal-fired plant (or conversion of an oil-fired station), and a detailed study to be undertaken on the desirability of a new nuclear power plant (probably a 1300 MW unit to be sited at Doel). The study, which will take at least two years to complete, will examine the economics of the scheme in detail, and construction of the station may not start until the study is complete.

Belgium nuclear capacity (GW)	
1978	1.7
1982	3.5
1985	4.5–5.5
1990	5.5
2000	5.5–8

Finland

Finland's indigenous supplies of energy are restricted to hydro, wood and peat, use of the latter being expected to grow significantly. In 1980 the total installed generating capacity was 9.3 GW of which 1.9 GW was hydro. However, major inroads have recently been made by nuclear power; 34% of electricity generation was met by nuclear plant in 1981, a figure which rose to 40.3% in 1982. This put Finland at the top of the world league table for the share of electricity generated by nuclear power.

Finland has four power reactors in operation, representing the full extent of the country's current nuclear commitment. Two of the reactors, sited at Loviisa and operated by the IVO utility, are Soviet-designed 440 MW (gross) PWRs. The construction of these reactors represents an interesting case study in technology transfer. The Soviet Atomenergo-export firm were responsible for supplying the main NSSS equipment but the operating utility was in charge of the design, purchasing and installation of the instrumentation and automation. This was realised in close cooperation with a number of diverse foreign companies from UK, Canada, France, FRG, Switzerland, and USA.

It is perhaps inevitable that this complex project, involving a large number of contractors from a significant number of different countries in both the East and the West, experienced difficulties and delays. The first unit, LO-1, was handed over to the utility in May 1977, ten months late, and the second unit, LO-2, was handed over in January 1981, two-and-a-half years behind the original schedule. However, compared with overall experience at nuclear construction sites throughout the world during this period, these delays do not appear untoward. Also, the excellent perform-ance achieved by both reactors as soon as they entered service is encouraging; during 1981 the LO-1 load factor was 80.6% and that of LO-2 70.5%. The corresponding figures for 1982 are 84.2% and 77.7%.

The two other reactors are at Olkiluoto and are owned by the TVO utility. The two identical plant units each have a net capacity of 660 MW and are equipped with Swedish ASEA-ATOM-type BWRs. The success of this development is even more impressive than at Loviisa. The first station, TVO-1, was connected to the national grid in September 1978, five years after excavation began; for TVO-2 the same stage was reached four years and ten months after the start of excavation. For both reactors, rated output was reached shortly after initial power-raising and subsequent performance has been consistently good.

With nuclear power meeting such a large proportion of electricity demand from just four reactors (TVO-1 and 2 together provided something like a quarter of Finland's electricity in 1982), periodic reductions in output due to limited baseload demand are not uncommon. Such a situation is seldom experienced in other countries having nuclear programmes, as maximum nuclear output is usually well below baseload demand.

It is difficult to explain satisfactorily the success of this modest Finnish nuclear programme. Given the limited nuclear expertise available in the country when the orders were placed, the fact that the two utilities opted for completely different reactor systems, and the harsh Finnish winters which inevitably pose extra problems during construction, it is a great tribute to the personnel involved, particularly those of the two utilities, that success has been achieved. It is perhaps necessary to examine the socio-economic structure of the country, particularly its close relationship to the Soviet Union, to explain this success. However, it is sufficient to note here that a rapidly growing economy, high rates of electricity demand growth and severely cold winters (which make thoughts of plant undercapacity untenable) have all made some contribution.

For the future, Finland's energy prospects are not unfavourable. Energy growth is likely to slow considerably as saturation effects, combined with a vigorous conservation programme, are felt. As far as electricity is concerned, studies are under way comparing the relative merits of coal, peat and nuclear for the next large power plant. If nuclear is thought to be the most attractive economically, it is likely that the two utilities IVO and TVO will cooperate on the construction of a single 1000 MW plant. Orders for such a station may be forthcoming by the end of 1984.

There is also a joint Finnish–Swedish project concerning the construction of a nuclear reactor for district heating purposes. A design for use in Helsinki, for example as 2×400 MW or 2×500 MW units, has been completed. In addition, Soviet reactors for district heating may be commercially available within the next few years.

Finland nuclear capacity (GW)	
1978	0.4
1982	2.2
1985	2.2
1990	2.2
2000	3–4

France

The energy picture in France is dominated by high oil imports and rapid growth in the use of nuclear power. Indigenous coal production is small (approximately 20 million tonnes annually) as is domestic production of natural gas. Hydro represents one of the most significant indigenous energy sources with 19 GW of installed capacity in 1980 (out of a total of 63 GW).

In 1978 oil imports accounted for 66% of all primary energy with the residential sector in particular being heavily dependent on oil products. By 1981 oil imports had fallen slightly in absolute terms and were down to 56% of total primary energy, but coal imports of 30 million tonnes made France the world's second largest coal importer after Japan. This strong dependence on imported fossil fuels, combined with the fact that electricity consumption per head is low in France compared with other industrialised countries, has led to a vigorous 'tout électrique' policy and a rapid development of nuclear power.

The original path for nuclear development chosen in France was similar to that adopted in the UK, namely the gas-graphite system (Magnox in the UK) which served the dual role of electricity generation and plutonium production. In the years from 1960 to 1972, 2.3 GW of these reactors were brought on line and some export orders were also won. The last of the gas-graphite reactors were in excess of 500 MW capacity, whereas in the UK it was only the twin Wylfa reactors which approached this size for a Magnox reactor.

In 1958 the Framatome company acquired a Westinghouse PWR licence and in 1960 won an order for the NSSS for a PWR at Chooz. This 300 MW plant was completed in 1967 and in the following year Framatome were given the order for the first European 900 MW PWR station, at Tihange in Belgium. In 1970 the French decided to concentrate on PWRs and in September of that year the order for Fessenheim I was given jointly to Framatome and the heavy-engineering firm of Creusot-Loire (which was a part owner of Framatome).

The first years of the 1970s saw an ambitious gamble by Framatome and Creusot-Loire. A rapid expansion of their engineering facilities, combined with a major increase in personnel, resulted in a manufacturing capacity of six nuclear units a year by 1972. However, in the years 1970 to 1973 EDF, the French electricity utility, placed orders for a total of just six nuclear units. With the advent of the oil crisis in the autumn of 1973, Framatome's fortunes improved and the years 1974–5 saw orders for thirteen units for the home market and a further two orders from Belgium. Further expansion of manufacturing facilities took place along with development of a 1300 MW nuclear system (the first orders in the 1970s were all for 900 MW units) and Framatome became established as the monopoly supplier in France.

From this early French commitment to PWRs, which only began in earnest in 1974, progress has been swift and impressive. The first 900 MW (nominal) unit came on-line in December 1977. By the end of 1982, 23 such reactors were operational and nuclear power was supplying 39% of France's electricity. At the same time, a further 27 reactors were at various stages of construction (eleven units of 900 MW, fifteen of 1300 MW, and a 1200 MW fast reactor), with three more (all 1300 MW) having approval for development. Framatome now no longer constructs reactors under licence from Westinghouse, as the expertise of licencee has overtaken that of licensor.

On gaining office in mid-1981, the Socialist Mitterrand Government called a halt to a development at five nuclear sites, so fulfilling an election pledge made to the French ecologist parties. However, far from representing a strong anti-nuclear position, the ensuing reassessment, which covered the whole energy spectrum, resulted in plans for continued growth in nuclear capacity, albeit at a slightly lower level than had been advocated by the previous administration. In fact, of the five sites frozen, only one (Le Pellerin) has been completely rejected, only to be replaced by a new site at Carnet, on the Loire. The identification of sites well in advance of need and the strategy of siting multiple units at one location, means that there should be little difficulty in obtaining sites for further nuclear expansion to the end of the century and beyond.

In addition to PWR development, France is now the acknowledged world leader in fast breeder reactor (FBR) technology. The 1200 MW Super-Phénix reactor at Creys Malville, which is due to come on-line in 1984, is twice the capacity of the world's next-largest fast reactor, the Soviet-built BN 600 situated at Beloyarsk in the USSR. There are no firm plans for further FBR development in the near future and it is likely that greater cooperation with other countries will be sought by the French before the start of any new FBR project (Super-Phénix is being built by EDF in cooperation with Italian and German utilities with part of its output being designated for Italian and German use in proportion to the financial commitment of the parties involved). Given the high capital cost of Super-Phénix and the low prevailing uranium price on world markets it is generally accepted that FBRs are not currently economically competitive with series-built PWRs.

Perhaps not surprisingly for a country which has a strong commitment to nuclear power and, perhaps as important, which is a nuclear weapons state, France has established a high degree of expertise in all areas of the nuclear fuel cycle. As far as mining is concerned, some economically recoverable uranium reserves exist in France itself (of the order of 60,000 tonnes) and there is significant activity by the state-controlled company Cogema in Niger. The Eurodif enrichment plant at Tricastin, a joint development by Cogema with companies from Italy, Spain and Belgium, reached its nominal output of 10.8 million separative work units (SWU) per year in 1981. The plant, using the highly electricity-intensive and, some believe, outdated, gaseous diffusion process, can provide the enriched uranium to fuel about 80 GW of nuclear power stations. In addition, France has extensive reprocessing facilities for PWR spent fuel at La Hague.

There has been significant opposition to nuclear power in France, some of which may be traced back to the violent student unrest of May 1968. One of the most disturbing protests took place at the Super-Phénix site at the end of July 1977. The large violent demonstration at the site and the brutal way in which participants were dealt with by crack French riot police had a profound effect on the local community.[13] Many concluded that nuclear power, whatever its risks, was preferable to having ugly riots at one's door-step. Since then opposition has become more restrained although, as has been noted, the Socialists felt it necessary to woo the not unsubstantial, anti-nuclear ecologists groups in the 1981 Presidential elections.

The lack of public debate in decision-making, the positive centrally planned energy strategy of successive French administrations, and the compensation paid to local people directly affected by nuclear projects (via both reduced tariffs and an annual tax, the *patente*, paid by EDF to the local community), have all served to negate the effect of nuclear opposition in France. It must also be pointed out that the short-lived slowdown on nuclear development, announced in 1981, was also met with violent protest by some members of pro-nuclear Communist trade unions who were concerned that unemployment might increase if rapid nuclear power development was not continued.

Given the status of reactors currently under construction or firmly planned, nuclear capacity estimates for 1985 and 1990 are not subject to great uncertainty, particularly as delays during construction have thus far been kept to a modest level. Even beyond 1990, specific plans concerning reactor ordering have been presented, although the extent to which these are implemented depends on future demand growth.

Perhaps the greatest uncertainty lies in the ability of French electricity consumers to increase demand sufficiently rapidly to utilise effectively the massive amount of nuclear capacity that will be available. During 1981, electricity demand continued to grow at approximately 6% per annum but nearly all of this increase may be attributed to the requirements of the Eurodif plant, which first attained full output during this period. Electricity consumption in 1982 was 261 billion kWh, just 1% higher than the 1981 figures. Nevertheless, it is likely that electricity demand will continue to grow at a faster rate in France than in many other European countries due to the present modest level of per capita consumption and a positive government commitment to electricity which will be backed by attractive tariff structures.

However, the situation may arise in which France has generating capacity far in excess of requirements, even with a vigorous push towards electricity. Any downturn in nuclear construction would have major political repercussions because of the significant implications for employment. One possibility is for France to export low-cost nuclear electricity to its near neighbours, something which is already happening to a limited degree, with Italy, in particular, receiving important quantities of electricity from France. (We develop further the whole theme of trade of nuclear electricity in Chapter 9.)

The overall picture indicates that with continued commitment to nuclear power at all levels of government and satisfactory performance of the completed stations during the next five years, nuclear capacity growth is likely to continue. There is certainly no doubt that the figures presented below are readily achievable by the extremely well-organised French nuclear industry.

France nuclear capacity (GW)	
1978	4.6
1982	23.3
1985	35–40
1990	50–56
2000	70–90

Federal Republic of Germany

The rapid growth in energy requirements in Germany during the post-war recovery period was largely met by increasing oil and gas imports. In 1950 solid fuel accounted for almost 90% of primary energy demand but by 1979 its share had fallen to below 30% and had declined slightly in absolute terms. Current German energy plans call for a substantial reduction in energy imports, particularly of oil.

Electricity supply in Germany is the responsibility of approximately 700 utilities which are generally private companies. The total installed generating capacity in 1980 was 82 GW, of which nearly 9 GW was nuclear and 6 GW hydro, the remainder being fossil-fuelled. At present 13% of electricity generation is produced by gas, much of it being used for baseload generation, with a further 5% coming from oil-fired plant. However, it is solid fuel which contributes most to electricity supply, with hard coal and lignite each accounting for about 30% of electricity production. Germany's lignite resources are sufficiently large to maintain present production levels of 130 million tonnes per year well into the next century. Lignite, as a non-premium, low-grade fuel is eminently suitable for use in power stations sited close to deposits and is likely to play an important part in electricity generation for the foreseeable future, although suggestions that it could better be used for producing gas, methanol or liquid hydrocarbons have also been made.

The main reactor vendor in Germany is the giant Kraftwerk Union (KWU). This company has expertise across the whole range of nuclear reactors and has successfully built both PWRs and BWRs at home and abroad (originally under licence from Westinghouse and General Electric). It has also exported its own design of pressurised heavy water reactor (PHWR) to Argentina, where Atucha 1 has operated very successfully, and is involved in the development and demonstration of a high temperature gas-cooled reactor (HTGR) for use as a source of process heat for industry. Significant development in fast reactor projects is also underway.

A second nuclear vendor is the Swiss/German Brown Boveri Company (BBC) which has offered PWRs built under licence from Babcock and Wilcox. However, this company has recently announced (spring 1983) that it has no plans to build any more LWRs, although it will maintain other interests in the nuclear field.

Nuclear capacity in Germany at the end of 1982 was almost 10 GW with a further 13 GW under construction, 6.6 GW of which is scheduled to be completed by the end of 1985. In addition, a further 12 GW of capacity is at the planning stage.

During the late 1960s and early 1970s German industry developed considerable nuclear expertise and quickly brought on stream a significant amount of nuclear capacity. In recent years, however, the original promise of nuclear power has not been realised and the morale of the industry is much lower than in France, for example. The reason for the change in fortunes is essentially twofold.

Firstly, the opposition to nuclear power in Germany has been amongst the strongest in the world. With a complex licensing process and the acknowledged right of protestors to challenge nuclear decisions in the courts, nuclear opponents have had considerable success in retarding progress. A second reason for the nuclear decline lies in revised forecasts of electricity demand made in the light of lower than expected growth rates during the 1970s (in common with other OECD countries). This, combined with the fact that Germany, with its indigenous sources of solid fuels, does not have the energy supply problems of France, has meant that there is no longer the pressing need for a massive nuclear programme, at least in the short term (this argument is reinforced by large cost overruns at nuclear sites and the prospect of significant quantities of low-cost natural gas from the Soviet Union). The most recent energy plans take full account of alternatives to nuclear power including coal-fired combined heat and power (CHP) stations, situated close to centres of demand.

However, there is some recent evidence to suggest that the fortunes of the nuclear industry are at last on the upturn. After five years of a de facto moratorium, construction permits were granted for three new 1300 MW stations in the second half of 1982. These three units are the first of a series of up to seven basically identical plants for which the licensing requirements, and their verification and certification by independent experts, have been closely harmonised. An important factor contributing to this upturn is pressure from the public to boost the economy through the promotion of private investment and the creation of additional jobs. The new Christian Democrat administration of Chancellor Kohl, with its favourable attitude to nuclear power, could also be important here.

Germany's nuclear problems have certainly not been completely solved and to assume that no more delays will occur in licensing and construction would be unreasonably optimistic. Consequently the capacity figures given below are substantially lower than industry figures presented as recently as May 1981.

Germany nuclear capacity (GW)	
1978	5.6
1982	9.8
1985	12.6–16
1990	19–23
2000	28–40

Italy

Italy, a country with very little indigenous energy and severe problems of plant undercapacity in its electricity network, appears ideally suited for the rapid development of nuclear power. In practice, however, progress in exploiting nuclear power has been extremely slow, principally because of problems in obtaining suitable sites.

In 1981, 85% of primary energy requirements came from imports, with oil imports alone accounting for 69% of total energy. In addition, significant quantities of both gas (principally from the Netherlands and the Soviet Union) and coal (from a number of diverse sources such as USA, Poland, South Africa and EEC countries) are imported.

The total installed electricity generating capacity in 1980 was 46.5 GW, of which approximately 29 GW was conventional thermal plant, nearly 16 GW hydro and 1.4 GW nuclear. Oil-fired plant accounts for over 55% of generation followed by hydro (28%), coal (9%), and gas (6%), with nuclear contributing less than 2%. Such a heavy dependence on oil for power generation is understandably of great concern to ENEL, the Italian electricity utility.

However ENEL's problems do not rest solely with an adverse mix of generating plant which results in heavy dependence on high-cost imported fuel. Lack of generating capacity is also a major difficulty. In 1981 net imports of electricity accounted for some 9.6 TWh (more than three times the output from Italy's nuclear stations), and by 1987 it is estimated that there will be a capacity shortfall of 7.7 GW at peak periods. With electricity demand growth in Italy continuing at a high level (averaging nearly 4% per annum in the period 1971–81), partly as a consequence of the present modest per capita consumption relative to other European countries, it appears that these problems will grow in the mid-term.

Current plans for medium-term capacity expansion call for an additional 10 GW of nuclear, 13.5 GW of coal, 1.8 GW of hydro, 1.13 GW of gas turbines and 0.1 GW of geothermal plant. Given the severe delays that have so far been encountered in obtaining permission to construct new power stations, it is unlikely that a significant proportion of this capacity will be on-stream by 1990.

Italy currently has one 860 MW BWR in operation at Caorso (supplied on a turnkey basis by the Italian company AMN in a joint venture with General Electric) plus three further small stations, one each of Magnox, PWR and BWR. The small (150 MW) BWR has now been shut down and the project officially terminated. In addition, construction began in 1979 on two 1000 MW BWRs at Montalto di Castro by the same consortium responsible for the Caorso reactor. Plans call for the first 6 GW of the

10 GW nuclear programme to be constructed as soon as possible. However, delays in finding suitable sites, caused by considerable local opposition from both the general public and regional council representatives at sites under consideration, have meant that progress has been slow. Recent developments in late 1982 and early 1983 point to some improvements and three sites have now been earmarked for development, with a possibility of two 1000 MW units (most likely to be Westinghouse PWRs) at each site. Construction will follow on-site investigations and is unlikely to start before 1985.

One of the reasons why regional councils have had an apparent change of heart over the siting of nuclear stations is a recent Italian law under which ENEL must compensate local communities for the socio-economic impact of new nuclear or coal-fired power stations. The compensation, which has two components, one related to electricity generation by the station and a second, once-and-for-all payment, related to installed capacity, is substantial. A 2 GW nuclear station might reasonably be expected to attract 45 billion lire (£21 million) to the local community over the lifetime of the station.

Given the present situation, the installed nuclear capacity to 1990 is constrained to remain at a low level. Post-1990 it is likely that nuclear power will start making a major contribution to electricity supply if only because there seem to be few alternatives. If major power supply interruptions become increasingly frequent towards the end of the 1980s, it is possible that some of the opposition to nuclear power will disappear and that a more pragmatic approach will be adopted by anti-nuclear campaigners. In the mid-term, electricity imports will become increasingly important. Italy is entitled to a one third share of the output of the 1200 MW Super-Phénix fast reactor in southern France, due for completion in 1984, in return for its contributions to the large investment required. ENEL will be hoping that the performance of this complex system is better than some observers think is likely during the early years of operation. Also, France has agreed to power transfers of 600 MW to Italy until 1985, corresponding to the French enrichment services booked but now not needed by Italy because of the delays in its nuclear programme.

Italy nuclear capacity (GW)	
1978	1.4
1982	1.3
1985	1.3
1990	2–3
2000	7–12

Netherlands

The principal source of indigenous energy in the Netherlands is natural gas, the country being the world's fourth largest producer (behind the USA, USSR and Canada). The huge Groeningen field supplies gas, via the European grid, to several countries in continental Europe. However, production from this field is expected to be declining by 1990, by which time gas from the Soviet Union will be meeting a significant proportion of European demand.

The total installed generating capacity in the Netherlands in 1980 was 19.7 GW, of which 0.5 GW was nuclear, the rest being fossil-fuelled. The bulk of generation comes from gas- and oil-fired plant (36% and 39% respectively in 1981) with an increasing contribution (19%) being met by coal-fired units. The remaining 6% of generation is met by the country's two operational nuclear reactors: a small, 50 MW, General Electric BWR which came on-line in 1969 and a 450 MW PWR, built by KWU of Germany, which was completed in 1973. There are no stations under construction.

A Government White Paper of July 1980 advocated construction of a further 3 GW of nuclear plant. However, the current public debate on energy is expected to last until mid-1983 and any nuclear capacity growth will come after 1990. An opinion poll held in 1980 showed that 49% of the public favoured cautious nuclear expansion, 12% wanted a crash programme and 36% were in favour of a complete ban, including a shutdown of the two operational reactors. Given the fairly substantial anti-nuclear feeling and recent downturn in electricity demand growth, it is unlikely that future nuclear capacity levels in the Netherlands will be high. The relatively small size of the supply network and the possibility of electricity imports from neighbouring countries both serve to reinforce this conclusion.

Netherlands nuclear capacity (GW)	
1978	0.5
1982	0.5
1985	0.5
1990	0.5
2000	0–3

Spain

Spain's principal indigenous energy resources are coal, hydro, uranium and offshore oil, the latter currently supplying approximately 10% of national requirements. Production of coal has increased significantly from 14.6 million tonnes in 1976 to 28.6 million tonnes in 1980 (some of this being low-grade coal). All natural gas is imported but some indigenous supplies have recently been discovered.

The rate of electricity growth has been the highest in Europe, averaging 7.9% per annum in the period 1969 to 1979. It is likely that future growth will continue at a high level of around 5% per annum to 1990 and 3% per annum to the end of the century. In 1980 the total installed generating capacity was approximately 30 GW, of which 13.5 GW was hydro. However, approximately two thirds of generation is met by conventional thermal plant with a little under 40% coming from oil- and gas-fired units. With much of the exploitable potential of hydro (around 20 GW) already utilised, future capacity expansion will be met by a mixture of coal and nuclear plant.

There are currently three first-generation nuclear stations in operation in Spain; one PWR (supplied by Westinghouse), one BWR (supplied by General Electric) and a gas-graphite reactor built in conjunction with France's Commissariat à l'Energie Atomique (CEA). The total installed capacity of these reactors, which came on-line between 1968 and 1972, is a little over 1 GW, the largest being the 480 MW gas-graphite reactor at Vandellos. The first of the second-generation reactors, the 930 MW Almaraz 1 Westinghouse PWR, came on-line in 1981, but problems with its steam generators (a generic problem common to generators of the D-3 type) have meant that full power operation had not been achieved by early 1983.

There are a further 11 reactors under construction (8 PWRs and 3 BWRs), nine of which were originally due to come on-line between 1976 and 1978. Six of the reactors are Westinghouse PWRs of around 930 MW each, two are KWU PWRs (1032 MW) and the three BWRs are all 975 MW General Electric units. However, significant delays in the programme have been experienced and the last of the 11 reactors will now not be on-stream until 1989 at the earliest. Construction at some of the sites is well advanced, with the Asco-1 reactor being at the power-raising stage at the beginning of 1983. Five more reactors are all planned to be operational by the end of 1985.

Of all the problems and delays which have been encountered at both the planning and construction stage, those at the Lemoniz I reactor will be highlighted as being perhaps the most bizarre and certainly the most unfortunate. The two Lemoniz reactors are being built in the Basque region of northern Spain. There has been considerable local opposition to the project and two successive chief engineers have been murdered by Basque separatists, most recently in May 1982. The Lemoniz I reactor is almost complete but it is likely that such acts will cause further, possibly extensive, delays and the future of the project is uncertain. It would be wrong to attribute these killings simply to strong anti-nuclear feelings in the Basque region as the complex political situation in the area extends far beyond differences of opinion on energy issues.

A further, potentially serious, setback to Spain's nuclear programme was the election in 1982 of the first Socialist government since the end of the Civil War. The new government has announced plans to limit nuclear capacity to 7.5 GW by 1990 and to boost the use of coal and natural gas, largely through increased imports. If these plans are implemented, work on five stations will be suspended. A further plant, on which initial site work had commenced and which was additional to the twelve second-generation units, is also likely to be axed. This latest energy plan differs significantly from that of the previous administration which, in December 1981, called for an installed nuclear capacity of 12.5 GW in 1990.

There is clearly a great deal of uncertainty surrounding future nuclear capacity levels in Spain, with technical problems, local opposition and the attitudes of future governments all likely to have some impact on the outcome. For this reason broad ranges for capacity figures, even to 1990 have been adopted.

Spain nuclear capacity (GW)	
1978	1
1982	2
1985	5–7.5
1990	7.5–11.5
2000	12.5–20

Sweden

With the exception of hydropower, Sweden has few indigenous energy resources and depends on imported oil for approximately 50% of total energy requirements. In 1980 the total installed electricity generating capacity was 27 GW, 14.5 GW being hydro, 8.5 GW conventional thermal and 4 GW nuclear. By the end of 1981 nuclear capacity was 6.5 GW and electricity generation figures for the same year show that hydro accounted for 58%, nuclear 37%, oil 5% and coal less than 1% of the total.

There are currently ten reactors in operation with a total capacity of 7.4 GW, the most recent being Ringhals 4, a PWR which has been plagued by steam generator problems. Of these reactors three are Westinghouse PWRs and the remainder are BWRs built by the Swedish company ASEA-ATOM. The BWRs are of interest because, unlike similar reactors operating in many other nuclear countries, they were neither built by, nor under licence from, General Electric and represent a completely independent Swedish development of the system. One of the most attractive features of the latest ASEA-ATOM BWR design is its inherent simplicity with coolant recirculation pumps being located inside the reactor vessel thus obviating the necessity for recirculation piping. As with all BWRs, no steam generators are required and it is argued that the simplicity of the overall system makes it particularly suitable for installation in countries with little nuclear expertise. The successful introduction of two of these reactors in Finland lends weight to this claim.

In addition to these ten operational reactors, two more are under construction (both Swedish BWRs), the last being scheduled for completion by the end of 1985. By 1990 nuclear power will account for over 40% of electricity generation.

Although the Swedish nuclear industry appears well placed to continue building power reactors for the home market, the future is far from clear due to significant public opposition to nuclear power. The nuclear question has become an important political issue and a referendum was held in March 1980 in an attempt to resolve the problem. Voters were presented with three options: line three was a 'no' vote which essentially rejected nuclear power out of hand and called for the decommissioning of all operational reactors within ten years – this attracted 38.5% of votes cast; line two was a cautious 'yes' vote which allowed for the operation of all twelve reactors already in service or under construction but which called for the decommissioning of these reactors after 25 years of operation and no further nuclear expansion – 39.3% of voters took this line; line one was similar to line two but showed a more open attitude towards further development of nuclear power in the future – supported by 18.9% of voters. A little over 3% of voters supported none of the options presented. The total turnout of voters was a high 74% of the adult population.

The 1980 referendum was a highly politicised debate with all major parties publicly supporting one of the three lines. For example, the Conservatives supported the pro-nuclear line one, while the strongly anti-nuclear line three was supported by the Centre Party, the Communists, some Social Democrats and Liberals as well as some civil servant organisations. There is clearly a significant, broadly based anti-nuclear feeling in Sweden, which will be of importance in determining future energy policy.

For the present analysis, the referendum results have made Sweden's mid-term nuclear future less uncertain than in many countries. By 1985 there will be between ten and twelve reactors in operation (depending on progress at Forsmark 3 and Oskarshamn 3). All twelve should be in service by 1990, by which time total nuclear capacity will be some 9.5 GW. By the year 2000 no additional reactors will be in service without a public change of direction on nuclear power. In addition, the early reactors will be reaching the end of their life by the end of the century and some will certainly have been retired if the 25-year limit for operation is enforced.

There is, however, recent evidence to suggest that anti-nuclear feelings are moderating somewhat as Sweden, along with France and Finland, becomes one of the European countries most dependent on nuclear power. The fact that Sweden's nuclear technology is largely home-grown and successful, further aids public acceptability. Nuclear district-heating schemes along with a low pressure, and inherently safer design of reactor may also contribute to a change of heart and, for this reason, the possibility of a modest increase in nuclear capacity between 1990 and 2000 is admitted in the high end of the ranges given.

Sweden nuclear capacity (GW)	
1978	3.7
1982	7.4
1985	7.4–9.5
1990	9.5
2000	7–12

Switzerland

Switzerland's only indigenous source of energy is hydro power. Out of a total installed electricity generating capacity of just under 14 GW in 1980, a little over 11 GW was hydro, 2 GW was nuclear, and thermal plant (oil-fired and peaking plant) totalled just 600 MW. With oil-fired plant providing only 1% of total electricity generation, Swiss power utilities have not been faced with the massive increases in fuel costs which have afflicted power companies in other OECD countries during the 1970s. In addition, growth in electricity consumption in the period 1969–79 averaged just 3.6% per annum, making it the second lowest growth rate in Western Europe after the UK (2.3% per annum).

There are currently four nuclear power stations operational in Switzerland. Three small stations were brought on-line between 1969 and 1972 employing US LWR technology (2 × 350 MW Westinghouse PWRs and one 320 MW General Electric BWR) and a further 920 MW PWR supplied by KWU entered service towards the end of 1979. Leibstadt, the fifth Swiss nuclear station, is currently at an advanced stage of construction and is due to be operational by 1984. This is a 940 MW General Electric unit of the latest BWR-6 family.

There has been growing opposition to nuclear power in Switzerland since the mid-1970s and formal objections raised at various stages of construction of the Leibstadt station have led to considerable delays in the project. There has also been fierce dispute involving the public, econo-mists and politicians over the necessity of proceeding with Kaiseraugst, a 955 MW BWR station which has been a component of long-term energy plans for several years. This project now has 'general permission' from the government to go ahead but final approval for commencement of con-struction rests with parliament and is unlikely to be obtained before the end of 1983. A further station, the Graben 1200 MW BWR, has not yet received 'general permission' to go ahead.

Following a referendum in May 1979, in which strong support was given to government proposals, it is now necessary to prove that the energy produced by any new nuclear station is necessary. Given the high standard of living enjoyed generally in Switzerland and the low energy intensity of its industries, it is likely that future growth in electricity demand will be modest. This ruling may therefore prove to be a significant hurdle in obtaining anything but modest growth in nuclear capacity.

Capacity figures to 1985 are constrained by those stations operational or under construction. For 1990, the upper capacity limit is obtained by assuming that the Kaiseraugst station is on-line, while the addition of the Graben station is thought to provide a limit to nuclear capacity to the end of the century.

It should be noted that Switzerland has a contractual entitlement to French nuclear capacity, currently put at 15% of the 2×890 MW Fessenheim station and 17.5% of Bugey 2 and 3 (2×925 MW). This type of arrangement, along with increases in electricity trade generally, may become increasingly important (as discussed in Chapter 9). Capacity figures given are for nuclear units sited in Switzerland only.

Switzerland nuclear capacity (GW)	
1978	1
1982	2
1985	3
1990	3–4
2000	4–5

United Kingdom

'Britain is self-sufficient in oil and gas, rests on a pile of coal, and is surrounded by cooling water.' Such was an assessment of the present UK energy situation made by a German participant at a recent interna-tional conference. There is little doubt that for a country of such small size and high population density, the UK is particularly well endowed with indigenous sources of energy. It is also possible that the very exist-ence of adequate indigenous energy sources has been a contributory factor to the extremely slow and painful development of nuclear power by a country which, in the early 1960s, enjoyed a position as world leader in the application of nuclear power for the large-scale supply of electricity.

In 1980 the total installed generating capacity in the UK was 76 GW, of which 67 GW was conventional thermal plant, 2.5 GW was hydro, and a little over 6 GW was nuclear. In the same year, nearly 73% of electricity generation was by coal-fired plant with just 13% being met by nuclear units. This heavy dependence on coal for electricity generation will continue well into the future even under the assumption of sustained nuclear expansion.

Commercial nuclear power development in the UK began with the Magnox programme, nine twin-reactor stations, totalling some 3.7 GW of capacity, being commissioned between 1962 and 1971. In 1965, after much debate, the advanced gas-cooled reactor (AGR) was chosen in preference to the US BWR system for Dungeness B, the first of the next generation of UK reactors.[14] There followed orders for a further four twin-reactor, 1200 MW stations representing a nuclear programme which may, at best, be termed problematic, at worst, disastrous. Significant delays were encountered at all five stations and by the end of September 1982 three were still not operational, including Dungeness B on which work started in 1965. By early 1983 these three stations had reached the initial stages of power-raising but were still being beset by problems. Doubts remain concerning the long-term performance levels which are likely to be achieved by these reactors.

There are several reasons why the AGR programme was a failure, among which the most important appear to be: insufficient design work completed before the start of construction, the awarding of contracts to weak consortia unqualified to undertake such large and complex projects, and the premature move from a 30 MW prototype reactor to a 600 MW commercial system. However, it is now thought that most of the problems of the AGR have been resolved and in 1978 two more orders were placed for AGRs at Heysham II and Torness. These reactors closely follow the design of Hinkley Point and Hunterston B, by far the most successful of the first five stations. Much has been learnt from problems encountered during construction of the first AGRs and progress to date at the two new sites appears to be proceeding according to schedule.

For the future, the CEGB, the utility responsible for electricity generation in England and Wales, has opted for a Westinghouse PWR at Sizewell B as the first of the next generation of nuclear reactors. However, before work can start on the project, CEGB proposals are being scrutinised at a far-reaching public inquiry, which started in January 1983. In addition to site-specific issues, problems such as PWR safety and the long-term need for generating capacity lie within the terms of reference of the inquiry. With recent criticisms of UK utility planning coming from government agencies and members of the academic establishment,[15,16] in addition to traditional pressure groups such as Friends of the Earth, the Sizewell B inquiry (five months old at the time of writing and due to continue well into 1984) is proving to be more than a mere formality.

Up to 1990, the upper limit to nuclear capacity is constrained by those reactors operational or under construction. By that time some of the original Magnox reactors will be more than 25 years old and may have been retired, depending on the position adopted by both the utilities (the CEGB in England and Wales and the SSEB in Scotland) and the independent Nuclear Installations Inspectorate (NII). By the year 2000, no Magnox reactors will be operational and a little under 8 GW of AGRs should be on-line. To this must be added all stations yet to be built (including Sizewell B, if approved), which will come on-stream during the 1990s and will probably all be PWRs. The most recent official estimates for nuclear capacity in 2000 for the whole of the UK (assuming just 1 GW in operation in Scotland) lie in the range 15 to 19 GW.[17] These figures assume medium economic growth (1% per annum real GDP growth to 2000) and either a medium or high nuclear background. Although the assumptions regarding economic growth cannot be criticised as being unrealistically optimistic, it is nevertheless felt that the overall range for nuclear capacity is too high.

Electricity demand growth in the UK during the 1970s has been lower than in any other Western European country and during the last four years has been virtually stagnant. With coal-fired plant as a viable alternative for baseload generation and utility plans for extending the lifetime of existing non-nuclear plant to 40 years, UK nuclear capacity figures in the year 2000 will, more realistically, lie in the range 10–17 GW. Even under favourable assumptions, Sizewell B is unlikely to be operational before 1993. The upper end of our range would require one reactor a year to be commissioned, following Sizewell, to the end of the century.

UK nuclear capacity (GW)	
1978	5.8
1982	5.8
1985	9
1990	10–11.5
2000	10–17

Other Western European countries

The remaining countries in Western Europe currently have no firm plans for nuclear development and none will have reactors operating by 1990. The countries are:

Denmark*	Cyprus
Iceland	Greece*
Ireland	Malta
Luxembourg	Portugal*
Norway	Turkey*

Those marked (*) are possible candidates for nuclear power in the mid-term (by 2000) as they are all heavily dependent on imported energy and have experienced high electricity demand growth of between 6% and 9% per annum in the period 1976–80. By 2020 Ireland and possibly Norway could be added to the list (it is assumed that Luxembourg will rely on imported nuclear electricity from neighbouring countries). Without making any detailed country-by-country analysis, it is suggested that the following capacity ranges represent plausible total nuclear figures for the ten countries listed above:

Other Western Europe nuclear capacity (GW)	
1978	0
1982	0
1985	0
1990	0
2000	3–10

OECD Pacific

Japan

Japan's only indigenous sources of energy are hydro power and a modest amount of coal (current production around 18 million tonnes per annum). Oil imports of 235 mtoe in 1981 were the second largest of any country in the world (after the USA at 287 mtoe). With a large population and high energy use per capita, problems of energy supply represent a significant constraint on future economic growth and, against this background, the rapid development of nuclear power is considered essential by the Japanese government.

The total installed electricity generating capacity in 1980 was 145 GW of which 29 GW was hydro, 14 GW nuclear and the remainder conventional thermal plant. In the same year oil-fired plant accounted for 40%

of the total of 578 TWh generated, with gas-fired plant contributing a further 14%. Nuclear-generated electricity has grown from 34 TWh in 1976 to 83 TWh in 1980.

Japan's first commercial nuclear station was the 160 MW Tokai-Mura Magnox reactor which came on-stream in 1966. This is the only gas-graphite reactor in the country and it was followed by reactors employing US LWR technology, the first of which began operation in 1970. Initially these stations were supplied on a turnkey basis by General Electric (BWRs) and Westinghouse (PWRs), but later units were built by the major domestic manufacturers with Hitachi and Toshiba being responsible for BWR construction (under licence from General Electric) and Mitsubishi building PWRs under licence from Westinghouse. These suppliers now possess, with few exceptions, the technical expertise and manufacturing capability to assume full responsibility for the total plant.

By mid-1983 there were 25 reactors operational with a total net capacity of 16.6 GW. In addition, there are a further eleven units under construction representing 10.3 GW of capacity and nine units (7.4 GW) at the planning stage, including a 300 MW fast reactor. Official government figures published in August 1979 estimated that nuclear capacity would amount to 30 GW in 1985, 53 GW by 1990 and 78 GW by 1995. These figures appeared unrealistically high when they were produced and the latest policy revision of the country's nuclear programme by the Ministry of International Trade and Industry sets a target of 46 GW of plant in service by 1990. Even this figure is unlikely to be achieved given the present status of site development.

The nuclear programme in Japan has not been without problems. The load factors achieved by LWRs have been significantly lower than was originally hoped for and, by the end of 1982, just three stations had cumulative load factors greater than 70%. There has also been considerable public opposition to nuclear power which has, on occasions, resulted in violent demonstrations. However, efforts have been made to ameliorate both problems: recently load factors for both PWRs and BWRs have been significantly better than those prevailing during the late 1970s, and a concerted programme of public education is underway which aims to increase the acceptability of nuclear power. The latter scheme is combined with government subsidies to communities in the vicinity of nuclear plants.

It should be noted that a very positive attitude to nuclear safety exists in Japan. This was demonstrated after the accident at Three Mile Island when Ohi 1, the only PWR in operation at the time, was shut down while overall safety was reassessed (this type of response to accidents is explored further in Chapters 4 and 5). Other PWRs, which were all undergoing regular inspection and refuelling, were also subjected to rigorous scrutiny.

A further problem which has aroused concern, particularly following the setting up in 1977 of the International Nuclear Fuel Cycle Evaluation (INFCE) at the instigation of US President Carter, is the heavy dependence on the US for LWR fuel. This dependence will continue at least to 1990 (although some deliveries of fuel enriched at the French Eurodif plant have been made), and is considered by the Japanese to be undesirable because of the severe restrictions which are attached by the US to fuel supply contracts, particularly with regard to reprocessing spent fuel. For this reason it is considered essential in Japan that independent expertise be acquired in all aspects of the nuclear fuel cycle from enrichment and fuel fabrication to final reprocessing. Work is even under way on the development of a plant for the extraction of uranium from seawater.

With such a heavy dependence on imported fossil fuel, Japan is reluctant to maintain a position whereby a single supplier, whose past actions have been somewhat fickle, must be relied upon for a steady supply of enriched uranium. A major issue here is Japan's commitment to fast reactors as the ultimate route to energy self-sufficiency implying, as it does, a move to large-scale local reprocessing, with the plutonium extracted being recycled in both LWRs and FBRs. Officially, nuclear capacity in the year 2020 is put at something like 320 GW, of which half will be fast reactors.

In estimating future nuclear capacity levels, a number of key points must be considered. All future stations will either be nuclear or coal-fired (relying on imported coal) as the only significant hydro development possible is in the form of pumped-storage schemes. Electricity growth has been extremely high in the past (12.7% per annum 1960–70, 5.1% per annum 1970–80) and is likely to remain fairly high as electricity is used to substitute for fossil fuels (official figures put electricity growth at 3.5% per annum during the period 1990–2000 and 1.75% per annum from 2000–20). Also, with nearly 100 GW of thermal plant in operation, most of which is oil- or gas-burning, there is likely to be a large requirement for nuclear plant for replacement purposes, even if demand growth is lower

Japan nuclear capacity (GW)	
1978	11
1982	17
1985	20–23
1990	27–33
2000	60–95

than currently predicted. Official capacity figures for 1990 appear over-optimistic (as does the figure of 320 GW for 2020), nevertheless, it seems inevitable that nuclear capacity will grow rapidly. The figures presented below take account of firm plans for the short term (to 1990), and realistic maximum rates of capacity expansion to 2000 (the official estimate for nuclear capacity at the end of the century is 90 GW).

Other OECD Pacific

This group consists of just two countries – Australia and New Zealand which, together with Japan, form the so-called JANZ region of OECD countries in the Pacific. Neither country has any firm plans for nuclear development and, even by the year 2020, nuclear capacity will be very small compared to that of Japan.

In 1980 the total generating capacity in Australia was 24.1 GW (17.6 GW of thermal plant, 6.5 GW of hydro) and in New Zealand was 5.9 GW (1.8 GW of thermal plant, 3.9 GW of hydro plus a small amount of geothermal). Given the very large quantities of indigenous coal in Australia and the significant untapped hydro reserves in New Zealand, there appears to be no pressing need for nuclear power. However, tentative plans exist for one 600–800 MW nuclear unit to be built in Western Australia to come on-line by 1995. It appears at present as if Australia's main role for the foreseeable future will be as a major supplier of natural uranium, particularly from the large new mines being developed in the Northern Territory, rather than as a supplier of nuclear reactor technology.

Australia and New Zealand nuclear capacity (GW)	
1978	0
1982	0
1985	0
1990	0
2000	0–2

Developing world

OPEC

The thirteen OPEC countries, which are listed below, will be considered collectively rather than on a country-by-country basis. By definition, the countries which form this select, and often misrepresented, group do not have the extreme energy supply problems, caused by heavy dependence on imported oil, which face some countries. Nevertheless, the

Table 2.3 *The OPEC countries*

Middle East and North African countries	Other countries
Algeria	Ecuador
Iran*	Gabon
Iraq*	Indonesia
Kuwait	Nigeria
Libya*	Venezuela*
Qatar	
Saudi Arabia	
United Arab Emirates	

* Countries which have, at some time, made plans for nuclear power

OPEC countries are extremely diverse and while Kuwait, for example, will have little difficulty in satisfying its own demand for energy well into the future, other countries such as Venezuela and Indonesia are faced with severe energy and economic problems in spite of the fact that they are currently net oil exporters.

In 1980 the total installed electricity generating capacity of all the OPEC countries was 31 GW, with 6 GW being hydro and the rest fossil-fuelled plant. Venezuela accounted for 9.1 GW of this total and Iran a further 5.3 GW, while many of the Gulf States have installed capacities of less than 2 GW. It is partly because of the very small size of the supply networks in some of the OPEC countries that nuclear power is unlikely to make major inroads in the foreseeable future; a general guideline adopted when considering system expansion is that the size of any one plant should not exceed 10 to 15% of the total firm capacity of the grid.[18] At present the smallest reactors commercially available are around 400 MW (for example the Soviet VVER-440 PWR system), which implies a minimum grid size of 2.5 GW before nuclear development can begin. A further major reason why nuclear power is inappropriate for many of these countries lies in their huge oil and gas reserves, only a fraction of which are required to fuel power stations to serve their relatively small populations (the present combined population of Qatar, UAE and Kuwait is less than 2 million).

Of the thirteen OPEC countries, those marked * represent countries which either currently have, or in the recent past had, firm plans for nuclear power. Iraq ordered a 900 MW PWR from France but the Israeli attack on their Tamuz 1 research reactor in June 1981, combined with the current hostilities with Iran, mean that it is now unlikely that a commercial-sized nuclear power station will be operating before the end of the century. Libya has ordered a 300 MW plant from the USSR for desalination and electricity supply but the suspicion with which this country is viewed by many Western nations points to possible problems concerning the training of adequate numbers of personnel. Venezuela has considered the use of nuclear-generated steam for heavy oil recovery and it has been suggested, in this context, that the Magnox reactor, with its relatively high steam temperature, may gain a new lease of life.

The Iranian nuclear programme, initiated in 1970, was ambitious by any standards and called for 23 GW of nuclear plant to be operational by 1992. Close links with German and French suppliers were formed and, when the revolution terminated the programme in 1978, one 1200 MW PWR supplied by KWU was 85% complete. It has recently been suggested that the cooling towers of the unfinished reactors be used as grain silos. Given the present political situation in Iran, no reactors will be operating by 1990 and it is considered extremely unlikely that nuclear power will make any contribution to electricity supply by the end of the century. (The Iranian episode helps to explain why nuclear capacity estimates made as recently as 1977 now appear hopelessly unrealistic, and may perhaps be used to emphasise the uncertainty surrounding the overall analysis presented in this chapter.)

For the long-term future some OPEC countries may turn to nuclear power to sustain high electricity growth (a consequence of present low per capita use of electricity and high population growth rates). The countries most likely to choose a nuclear future are Indonesia, Venezuela and Ecuador with Algeria, Iraq and Libya being further long-term possibilities.

OPEC nuclear capacity (GW)	
1978	0
1982	0
1985	0
1990	0
2000	0–2

Argentina

Argentina is fortunate among developing countries in that it is virtually energy self-sufficient. In 1979 overall domestic production accounted for 91% of total energy requirements with production of petroleum and its derivatives meeting just over 92% of demand. Total electricity generating capacity in 1980 was just under 12 GW; 8 GW of thermal plant, 3.3 GW of hydro and a small nuclear component. The part played by coal in electricity generation is negligible, oil and gas being the major fuels for thermal plant. By the year 2000, the use of oil in the electricity sector is expected to be half the 1979 level of 194 PJ, while gas use for electricity generation will increase in the same period from 130 to approximately 200 PJ.[19]

There is currently one nuclear reactor in operation in Argentina, the 367 MW (gross) Atucha 1 reactor sited at Lima, 110 km north-west of Buenos Aires. This reactor began commercial operation in June 1974, having been supplied on a turnkey basis by the German company Siemens, and has proved extremely successful in operation with a cumulative load factor, to the end of 1982, of 75% (this makes it one of the world's most successful power reactors). Two further reactors are under construction; a 600 MW Candu reactor is being built at Embalse in the Province of Cordoba by a Canadian–Italian consortium, AECL-IT, and a second reactor of 700 MW capacity is being built at the Atucha site to a KWU design.

All three reactors use heavy water as coolant and moderator with natural uranium fuel. However, only the Embalse reactor is of the conventional (pressure-tube) Candu design. The German-designed reactors, Atucha 1 and 2, have a single pressure vessel through which fuel tubes pass, and the coolant and moderator (both D_2O) are kept at equal pressure (but not equal temperature) within the reactor pressure vessel. In this way the Atucha reactors represent a reactor concept with features common to both the Candu and the PWR. As with the Candu, refuelling is performed on-load, but the vertical fuel channels of the Atucha reactors require that refuelling be performed from above the reactor rather than from the side, as is the case for the Candu with its horizontal pressure tubes.

The degree of Argentinian participation in construction of the three reactors has increased from 33% for Atucha 1 to a projected 62% for Atucha 2. In fact, Atucha 2 is the first of the three stations not to be built on a turnkey basis, with domestic supplies and services for the plant being the responsibility of the national atomic energy commission (CNEA). The reactor at Embalse is due to begin commercial operation during 1983, while Atucha 2 is due to come on-stream in 1988.

Argentina also has plans for complete independence in the nuclear fuel cycle. Local uranium resources are being utilised (reasonably assured reserves of 30,000 tonnes U_3O_8 have been established) and an industrial fuel fabrication plant was inaugurated in April 1982. As the Argentinian reactors use natural uranium fuel, no enrichment plant is necessary, but a pilot scale reprocessing plant is at an advanced stage of construction with full operation scheduled for mid-1984. Natural uranium/heavy water reactors produce significant quantities of fissile plutonium, particularly when operated on a short dwell-time fuel cycle. For this reason the reprocessing plant has been viewed with strong suspicion in some quarters where it is thought that the real purpose of the plant is to provide Argentina, which is not a signatory to the Nuclear Non-Proliferation Treaty (NPT), with plutonium for a weapons programme.[20] In addition to these facilities, a 2 tonnes/year pilot heavy water production plant is at an advanced stage of construction and is expected to start operation in 1983.

Official government plans call for the construction of three additional reactors (each of 1 GW), all of which are due to be operational by the end of the century. There are a number of reasons why these plans may not be realised, however, in spite of the relative success of the programme to date. Firstly, Argentina has significant quantities of hydro reserves which have yet to be exploited (current plans call for a further 25 GW of hydro capacity by 2000). Secondly, it is far from clear that future demand justifies this large programme of capacity expansion, implying, as it does, very high levels of economic growth. Finally, the severe economic problems of Argentina with hyper-inflation and large foreign debt levels indicate that there could be significant problems in financing further nuclear projects. For this reason it is thought that 2 GW represents an upper bound on capacity expansion to the year 2000 (in addition to the three stations in operation or under construction), with 1 GW representing a not unlikely outcome.

Argentina nuclear capacity (GW)	
1978	0.4
1982	0.4
1985	1.0
1990	1.7
2000	2.7–3.7

Brazil

The principal indigenous source of commercial energy in Brazil is hydropower which, in 1977, accounted for 23% of primary energy input. Also important is non-commercial fuel (wood and bagasse), accounting for 27% of primary energy input, along with petroleum and its derivatives. The latter accounted for 42% of primary energy in 1977, 82% of which was imported. Installed electricity generating capacity has grown rapidly from just over 6 GW in 1963 to nearly 32 GW in 1980, 86% of this capacity being provided by hydro plant.[21]

In the mid-1970s Brazil embarked on an ambitious nuclear programme at a time when electricity growth was in excess of 11% per annum. By

1981, however, electricity demand growth was down to 3.3% per annum as industrial production fell and the economy shrank. In the São Paulo industrial region electricity demand actually fell in 1981 and resulted in a 15% surplus of generating capacity. Against this background the original nuclear programme has been substantially reduced.

At present, just one reactor is operational, the troubled Angra 1 station. This is a 626 MW Westinghouse PWR which, by April 1982, was operating on test at low power, six years behind schedule. A second station, Angra 2, is currently under construction and is due to start production in 1988. This is a 1300 MW (nominal) PWR supplied by KWU and represents the first stage of an ambitious Brazilian–German joint venture in which a series of 8 PWRs, all of 1300 MW, are to be built to German design. The degree of Brazilian involvement is expected to increase with each station until technology transfer is complete and Brazil is able to compete in world markets for orders for the major parts of the nuclear island. Construction of Angra 3, the second 1300 MW station, is due to begin in 1984.

In addition to reactor construction, plans exist to exploit Brazil's significant uranium reserves (currently put at around 230,000 tonnes U_3O_8 with much of the country yet to be prospected), and to develop enrichment facilities. A jet-nozzle uranium enrichment plant is currently under construction, again using German expertise, and output is expected to reach 300 tonnes separative work by 1988. In this way Brazil is aiming for complete independence in the nuclear fuel cycle, a prospect viewed with concern in some areas as Brazil is another Latin American country which is not a signatory to the NPT.

Although this programme of technology transfer is still viewed enthusiastically in Germany, there is increasing evidence of disillusionment on the side of the Brazilians. The high perceived cost of the programme has helped to turn both government and the public away from nuclear power. A further problem lies in the present high levels of foreign debt in Brazil which would be severely exacerbated by continued rapid nuclear development. The indebtedness of Brazil, along with several other Latin American countries (notably Mexico and Argentina) has now reached such high levels that real concern is being expressed in international financial circles that some countries may actually default on their debts, the consequences of which would be felt worldwide.

To these problems must be added the current, lower than anticipated, growth in electricity demand and the rapid growth in hydro capacity, which is proceeding in parallel with the nuclear programme. The Itaipu hydro scheme on the Brazil–Paraguay border will be the largest in the world when it is commissioned in 1983–4, with its capacity of 12.6 GW being shared between the two countries involved. However, there is considerable doubt as to Paraguay's ability to absorb this additional capacity and it is likely that Brazil will take more than 50% of the plant's output in return for payments and/or other aid to Paraguay.

The full programme of eight reactors (in addition to Angra 1) would, if implemented, lead to a total installed nuclear capacity of around 11 GW by 2000. However, three of these stations are due to come on-line between 1998 and 2000 and any downwards revision of the programme, or time overruns during construction, would reduce the programme substantially. For the present work it will be assumed that nuclear capacity in 2000 is unlikely to exceed 7 GW, particularly as work on the fourth and fifth units of the programme was suspended indefinitely towards the end of 1982. With the hydro and nuclear projects, and an ambitious alcohol-from-biomass programme, all being heavily capital intensive, project financing is likely to remain a severe constraint for the foreseeable future.

Brazil nuclear capacity (GW)	
1978	0
1982	0.6
1985	0.6
1990	2–3
2000	4.5–7

Egypt

Egypt's two major sources of indigenous energy are oil and hydro. In 1980 crude oil production was over 29 million tonnes, a little under 6 million tonnes of which was exported. Hydro capacity in the same year was 2.6 GW (out of a total installed capacity of 4.5 GW) and accounted for 52% of total generation. Nearly 50% of the installed generating capacity was met by one project, the 2.1 GW High Aswan dam which first began operation in 1967. In common with many other developing countries, electricity growth has been very high, averaging 7.7% per annum in the period 1970–9, although the downturn in the economy towards the end of the 1970s was reflected in a fall in demand growth to just 2.6% per annum between 1977 and 1979.

There are currently no nuclear power stations either in operation or under construction in Egypt but the country's nuclear plans are ambitious. Agreements have been signed with both the US and France for the supply of two 1000 MW nuclear units and negotiations are also in hand with the Federal Republic of Germany for up to four more units. This would give a maximum installed capacity of around 8 GW to be in service by 2000.

Before embarking on such a programme it is essential that a developing country should acquire some expertise in the general area of nuclear engineering. This has been recognised in Egypt, which is now the most advanced Arab country with regard to the training of nuclear engineers. Courses are offered in Egyptian universities to students who wish to pursue a career in nuclear engineering, either at degree or at technical level. In addition, a significant amount of fundamental nuclear research is being undertaken locally by highly qualified specialists using a variety of sophisticated experimental and theoretical techniques.

Nevertheless significant problems exist which make the goal of 8 GW of nuclear power by 2000 appear over-optimistic. Perhaps most importantly, it is far from certain that future electricity demand growth justifies a programme of this size. Even if such a programme were desirable, a major difficulty regarding the integration of 1000 MW nuclear units into what is, at present, a small and weakly consolidated grid system would have to be overcome. Notwithstanding these problems, there remains the difficulty of financing a large capital intensive programme for a country with constraints on foreign exchange. In practice continued reliance on oil-fired power stations may be difficult to avoid.

Egypt nuclear capacity (GW)	
1978	0
1982	0
1985	0
1990	0
2000	2–5

India

India's principal sources of indigenous energy are hard coal (annual production 79 mtce in 1980) and hydro. Although oil production is not negligible, imports account for more than 50% of total requirements for crude oil and petroleum products. In the electricity sector the total installed capacity of around 34 GW in 1980 was met by 20.7 GW of conventional thermal plant (principally coal-fired), 12.3 GW of hydro plant and a little over 600 MW of nuclear plant. Hydropower is a vital component of electricity supply, meeting 40% of total generation in 1980, but it is also highly variable, depending as it does on the monsoon rains. As far as coal is concerned, the large distances from mines to centres of demand, combined with the high ash content of the fuel, have resulted in high generation costs and help to explain the positive move to nuclear power that is now underway in India.

The first nuclear station, at Tarapur, consists of two 200 MW General Electric BWRs which came on-line in 1969. This was the only station employing LWR technology and all subsequent reactors have concentrated on natural uranium, heavy water systems. Rajasthan 1, the first Candu reactor, of 207 MW capacity, came on-line in 1973 with a second similar reactor, Rajasthan 2, being completed in 1981. Four more units are under construction, each of 220 MW capacity (Madras 1 and 2; Narora 1 and 2) and a further ten reactors of similar design are planned, the site for the first two having already been chosen and preliminary work initiated.

India is currently the only country in the world still pursuing commercial power reactors of such small size.[22] With the smallest reactors available in commercial markets being upwards of 400 MW, it is conceivable (though perhaps unlikely) that India could eventually export 200 MW PHWRs to other developing countries with small electricity grids.

For the future, a move to 500 MW units is envisaged with a series of 12 due for completion by the end of the century. This would give a total installed capacity of 10 GW by 2000, excluding a small fast reactor due to be operational in 1983.

This nuclear programme has not, however, been without problems. In 1974 India exploded its first atomic bomb and, at a stroke, lost much of the goodwill and cooperation that had been built up with supplier countries, particularly Canada. This is one of the reasons why Indian manufacturers were responsible for the majority of the Rajasthan 2 station (the Canadian involvement in Rajasthan 1 was substantial). It also helps to explain the dismal performance of both Rajasthan reactors as Indian engineers were no longer able to call on the considerable Canadian expertise in the field of PHWR technology to help resolve problems.

Furthermore, India's difficulties have not been confined to the Rajasthan reactors. Since December 1980 no supplies of enriched uranium fuel for the two Indian BWRs has been forthcoming from the US. Agreement has now been reached with France for the supply of enriched uranium hexafluoride, after much wrangling over the thorny problem of non-proliferation safeguards, and first deliveries are scheduled for mid-1983.

A further problem lies in the supply of heavy water. Three plants are currently in operation, with a total output of approximately 200 tonnes of heavy water per year. However, each 220 MW reactor under construction requires an initial heavy water inventory of 250 tonnes and, with losses from operational reactors being significant due to the large number of outages, shortages have become a major problem. The Madras 1 reactor has been delayed partly because of insufficient heavy water, although it now appears that supplies may be forthcoming from the

Soviet Union. Links with the Soviet Union would be further increased if India elected to build two 440 MW Soviet PWRs, an option which has been under consideration for some time.

The Indian commitment to nuclear power is strong, but many of the problems that have been encountered in its ambitious programme may be traced, either directly or indirectly, to the mistrust with which suppliers of nuclear technology view a developing country which has refused to sign the NPT, operates an unsafeguarded reprocessing plant, and has actually detonated a nuclear device.

In estimating the installed nuclear capacity to the end of the century, it is necessary to consider to what extent present problems will persist and in what way they are likely to modify existing plans. One of India's main aims is to achieve complete independence in the nuclear fuel cycle (including reprocessing) and in the production of heavy water. A further priority will be the elimination of design and engineering defects in future reactors such that reasonable plant load factors may be achieved. With the majority of the overall programme being implemented by local suppliers there will not be the severe problems related to project financing that have plagued nuclear programmes in Latin American countries. Nevertheless, the scale of the programme is such that a significant amount of scarce resources will have to be earmarked for nuclear purposes.

As far as electricity demand growth is concerned, the rate of 7% per annum in the period of 1970–9 (which was maintained in the years 1977–9), combined with very low per capita use and a large and expanding population, all indicate that the planned 10 GW of nuclear plant by 2000 is not excessive. It will be assumed that this figure represents an upper bound for the end of the century with a reasonable lower bound being 7 GW (representing delays to six of the planned 500 MW units, possibly due to constraints on the supply of heavy water).

India nuclear capacity (GW)	
1978	0.6
1982	0.8
1985	1.3–1.5
1990	1.7–2.6
2000	7–10

Republic of Korea

Korea's main indigenous energy source is coal, with total production in 1979 amounting to 18 million tonnes of hard coal plus a further 10 million tonnes of low-grade coal. This coal is principally used in industry

(particularly the iron and steel industry) rather than for electricity generation, and it is oil-fired plant which meets the greatest part of power
generation, with hydro supplying just 6% of demand.[23] The total
installed generating capacity in 1980 was just over 10 GW, of which
1.2 GW was hydro, 560 MW nuclear and 8.5 GW conventional thermal
plant. Growth in electricity demand has been extremely high, averaging a
little over 16% per annum in the period 1970–9. With high-cost imported
oil currently being used extensively for electricity generation, the Korean
government has embarked on a major nuclear programme to meet future
growth in demand.

By mid-1983, three nuclear stations were operating in Korea. The first, a
560 MW Westinghouse PWR came on-line in 1978 and has recently been
followed by a 630 MW Candu reactor and a second Westinghouse PWR of
similar capacity. There are a further six stations under construction, all
three-loop PWRs (of 900 MW nominal capacity). Four are Westinghouse
units, the other two being supplied by the French manufacturer Framatome.

To date, technology transfer to Korea appears to have proceeded well,
with local input to projects increasing with the number of stations under
construction. There is some British involvement in the programme; the
first four PWRs have used British–GEC turbo-machinery and have been
built as a joint turnkey project by Westinghouse and GEC, also the Candu
reactor was supplied jointly by AECL and the British concern Northern
Engineering Industries–Parsons. A plant is also under construction for the
manufacture of NSSS components under licence from Combustion
Engineering.

Official government plans made in the late 1970s called for 14 GW of
nuclear capacity to be installed by 1991 and up to 80 GW by the end
of the century. These figures now appear hopelessly optimistic. It has
recently been announced in Korea that the next four nuclear power units,
numbers 11 to 14 (there is no unit 4 as the number 4 is thought to be
unlucky), will be postponed for approximately one year because of a
downward revision of future demand. This means that a maximum figure
for installed nuclear capacity in 1990 is 7.2 GW which represents the
total net capacity of those stations either operating or under construction. Although it has been stressed officially that the last two PWRs under
construction (the French reactors, units 9 and 10) are not in jeopardy,
delays cannot be ruled out, particularly as construction is at an early
stage, and a lower bound on nuclear capacity in 1990 is obtained by
assuming that these units are not available.

Looking further into the future, nuclear power will become an increasingly important component of the Korean energy picture and could
account for more than 50% of all plant construction (the rest being

predominantly coal-fired plant). With little local opposition to nuclear power and limited scope for further hydro development, the actual nuclear capacity levels will be largely determined by growth in electricity demand which, in turn, depends, among other things, on population growth rates. Between 1965 and 1978 the population growth rate was a little over 2% per annum, the population in 1978 being approximately 37 million. The other key determinants in estimating future nuclear capacity lie in the ability of Korea to continue financing capital-intensive projects, and the possible competition to nuclear power from low-cost imported coal. The nuclear figures presented below, although high, are not considered unreasonable for a country such as Korea which combines high economic growth with strong central government control of energy and economic planning.

Korea nuclear capacity (GW)	
1978	0.6
1982	0.6
1985	1.8–3.6
1990	5.4–7.2
2000	11–18

Mexico

Mexico is an energy-rich country which nevertheless faces serious economic problems, with foreign debt currently running at unprecedented levels (around $70 billion in mid-1982). The recent fall in worldwide demand for oil, along with a softening of the oil price, has led to a reduction in the value of the peso which, in turn, has led to difficulties in servicing this debt. A further major problem facing the country is the very high rate of population growth which is expected to result in a population increase from 65.5 million in 1979 to 120 million by the end of the century.

The 1970s saw a rapid upturn in proven reserves of fossil fuels and a corresponding increase in local production of oil, gas and coal. In the electricity sector the total installed capacity in 1980 was 17.3 GW, of which 11.8 GW was conventional thermal plant and 5.3 GW hydro. As far as electricity generation is concerned, 25% was met by hydro plant (again 1980 figures) while a mixture of fuel oil, gas and diesel plant accounted for the remainder (coal is currently not used for power generation). The estimated maximum ultimate potential for hydro is 56.4 GW, with 12.5 GW planned to be in operation by 1990.

Against this background it is perhaps surprising that Mexico decided to embark on a large nuclear programme which called for the construction of some 22 GW of nuclear capacity by the end of the century. The programme began in 1969 with the order of a 1300 MW nuclear station, comprising two General Electric BWRs, at a time when the full extent of Mexico's fossil fuel reserves was not known. The continued justification of the programme rested on the low generating costs of nuclear stations and the need to conserve indigenous fossil fuels, particularly oil, to minimise resource constraints which are likely to be felt after the turn of the century. An additional factor lay in the not inconsiderable uranium reserves in Mexico, believed, in 1980, to be in the region of 10,000 tonnes.

To date, the programme has not been a success. The first nuclear station, at Laguna Verde, was due to begin operation in 1977 but prolonged delays have meant that fuel loading of the first reactor is now scheduled for 1985, with the second unit following about a year later. Tenders had been invited for the construction of a second nuclear station, but in May 1982 it was announced that all bids had been returned unopened to the seven vendors and the programme was indefinitely postponed.

This change of heart is a result of Mexico's economic problems, with the capital-intensive nuclear programme leading to severe difficulties with project financing. This has been exacerbated by the significant real increases in nuclear capital costs in recent years as safety requirements have increased in a declining world market. For the future, nuclear capacity in 1990 will be restricted to the 1.3 GW currently under construction. A recent independent assessment, made just before the latest setback of May 1982, estimated that installed nuclear capacity by the year 2000 will be 7 GW.[24] Given the present situation, however, it is thought that this will be an upper limit for year 2000 capacity and that more attention will be given to further development of hydro and coal-fired power stations, both of which pose less severe balance of payments problems than does a nuclear programme.

Beyond the end of the century there appear to be two possibilities: either financial constraints, high nuclear capital costs, and increases in proven coal reserves will lead to an energy future in which nuclear plays a minor role; or possible constraints on indigenous energy supplies combined with a more favourable economic climate and a worldwide improvement in nuclear economics and performance will provide a firm base for an accelerating programme beyond 2000. In any event, significant new generating plant construction of some type will be required if per capita consumption is to remain at the present modest (and highly non-uniform) levels, given the present rate of population growth.

Mexico nuclear capacity (GW)	
1978	0
1982	0
1985	0–1.3
1990	1.3
2000	3–7

Philippines

There are more than 7000 islands in the Philippines with a total population in 1978 of some 46 million. The population is growing rapidly (the average growth rate was nearly 3% per annum in the period 1965–78) and there are currently 21 cities with more than 100,000 inhabitants, located largely on the two main islands of Luzon and Mindanao. However, the total installed generating capacity in 1980 was just 4.6 GW, of which 950 MW was hydro, with the remainder being principally oil-fired plant. Geothermal power has recently started to make inroads (1980 capacity 446 MW), and it has been estimated that installed geothermal capacity by the end of the century could reach 4.4 GW.[25]

At present the Philippines are heavily dependent on oil imports but indigenous production is growing and in 1979 accounted for 10% of domestic consumption. Substantial reserves of low-grade coal exist, the production of which has been so developed that in 1977 supply exceeded local demand. It is planned to use this coal for power generation and in the cement and sugar-milling industries. The ultimate exploitable hydro reserves are put at 8.4 GW and development is currently being pushed vigorously in a programme which aims at 70% hydro utilisation by 2000.

Plans for nuclear power were originally proposed in the late 1960s and a firm commitment was made following the first oil price rise in 1973. Construction of the first station, a 620 MW PWR supplied on a turnkey basis by Westinghouse, began in March 1976 with commercial operation scheduled for 1985. The possibility exists of building a second similar reactor at the same site (near the city of Morong on the island of Luzon) but it seems unlikely that this option will be pursued in the near future.

It is interesting to contrast two divergent views of the Philippine nuclear programme, both of which were published in 1982. On the one hand,[26] the programme is presented as a successful case study in technology transfer, with an oil-dependent developing country obtaining a new and economic source of energy for the benefit of the population at large.

The alternative viewpoint[27] exposes the whole project as a high-handed, and at times unnecessarily secret, deal between the American

Westinghouse Corporation and the all-powerful President Marcos. (The latter had little difficulty in coping with any dissent, as the Philippines were under a state of martial law from September 1972 to early 1981.)

There has clearly been a great deal of opposition to the project locally and the whole issue has attracted substantial comment both in the US and Europe. Much of the concern has focussed on the safety of what, in some quarters, is presented as an outdated design, sited in an area of high seismic activity. Notwithstanding these objections, the overall economics of the scheme appear, at best, marginal and doubts must be raised as to whether nuclear power represents a timely and appropriate solution to the real energy and economic problems of the Philippines. For the present work we assume that the single nuclear unit is completed (although this appears far from certain in mid-1983), and that a maximum of one more unit of similar size will be operational by the end of the century.

Philippines nuclear capacity (GW)	
1978	0
1982	0
1985	0–0.6
1990	0.6
2000	0.6–1.2

South Africa

South Africa has major indigenous supplies of hard coal and uranium and depends on its Sasol (oil from coal) plants for much of its requirements for petroleum products. The total installed generating capacity in 1980 was 18.6 GW, most of which was coal-fired plant (hydro accounted for just 755 MW of capacity). Electricity demand growth is currently around 9% per annum and capacity shortages have caused major supply disruptions during recent winters.

There are two nuclear reactors under construction at present, due for completion in 1983 and 1984 respectively. The reactors, Koeberg 1 and 2, are 920 MW PWRs supplied by the French manufacturer, Framatome, and appear to have been built largely to cost and time.

The initial fuel charge for the first reactor has been supplied by France. However, the construction of a gas-nozzle enrichment plant at Valindaba points to South Africa's intention of becoming independent of foreign suppliers in all aspects of the nuclear fuel cycle, a situation which is perhaps not unexpected given the political isolation of the country.

The country's vast coal reserves will be used increasingly for power generation as installed capacity grows but there is also a possibility of additional nuclear stations being built in the Eastern Cape and Natal provinces, both being significant load centres remote from the coal reserves. Given that coal has to be used to produce liquid fuels and will also provide a long-term source of export revenue, an expansion of the nuclear programme has much to commend it from a South African viewpoint, particularly as the experience gained with France in transferring nuclear technology has been encouraging.

For the future it is thought that electricity demand growth will continue at a high level (around 5% per annum to the end of the century) and that nuclear units will be used to meet up to 20% of new capacity requirements.

South Africa nuclear capacity (GW)	
1978	0
1982	0
1985	1.8
1990	1.8
2000	3–6

Taiwan (Republic of China)

Taiwan has achieved rapid economic growth during the 1970s, averaging 10% per annum in the period 1974–9. However, energy consumption has been rising considerably faster than the gross domestic product of the country and heavy dependence on imported oil has led to considerable economic problems following the oil price rises of 1973 and 1979. Indigenous energy sources are limited (oil and gas reserves are small), but further hydro development is possible and an appreciable quantity of high-cost coal is thought to be available.

In 1980 the total installed generating capacity was a little over 8 GW (4887 MW oil-fired; 1208 MW nuclear; 1192 MW hydro; 866 MW coal-fired) with 59% of total generation coming from oil-fired plant. Electricity demand growth has been very high, averaging 13% per annum in the period 1974–9, and official utility estimates suggest that growth will continue at more than 6% per annum to the end of the century. It is planned to meet this demand by continuing the programme of nuclear development along with the construction of additional coal-fired plant, conversion of oil-fired power stations to coal-burning, and the development of further hydro sites (including pumped-storage schemes). A recent (February 1982) consultants' report estimates that total capacity in 1999 will be 31 GW, of which nearly 16 GW will be nuclear.[28]

By the end of 1982, two nuclear power stations were in operation, both twin-unit General Electric BWRs. The Chin-shan reactors ($2 \times 600\,MW$) came on-line in 1978 and 1979, and were followed first by Kuosheng 1, which entered service in late 1981, and then, a year later, by Kuosheng 2 (both $950\,MW$). A further station, Maanshan, is under construction comprising twin, $907\,MW$, Westinghouse PWRs, due for completion in 1984 and 1985.

Following this first stage of nuclear development, Taipower (the Taiwan utility) was, in 1980, planning for a second stage of six $900\,MW$ units to enter service between 1988 and 1993, followed by a further twelve $1200\,MW$ units which would be operational by the end of the century. This would provide a total installed nuclear capacity of nearly $25\,GW$ by the year 2000 (significantly greater than the 1982 estimate of $16\,GW$ discussed above).

It now appears unlikely that either of the above estimates for year 2000 nuclear capacity will be realised. In mid-1982 Taipower started to place contracts for a fourth nuclear station (capacity $2 \times 900\,MW$). The orders (for turbine-generators placed with Northern Engineering Industries–Parsons of England) were placed on a very long lead-time with commissioning of the first unit due in 1991, but they have since been cancelled and it is now uncertain when the station will be built. The reasons for cancellation are the lower than expected demand growth (electricity consumption actually fell in 1981), and severe economic problems which have led to difficulties in financing high-cost projects.

Taiwan nuclear capacity (GW)	
1978	0.6
1982	3.1
1985	3.1–4.9
1990	4.9
2000	7.5–14

Nuclear capacity to 1990 will now be limited to those units in operation or under construction with further additions not coming on-line before 1995. The development of nuclear power to the end of the century and beyond depends crucially on the extent to which the Taiwanese economy recovers from its present difficulties (which must be viewed in the overall context of a deep recession in the Western world). Previous forecasts have been over-optimistic and recent suggestions of commercial-sized fast breeder reactors being incorporated into the electricity network before the end of the century are not realistic. Also, with a population of around 18 million (growing at less than 2% per annum) demand saturation effects may become important before the end of the century and have possibly been underestimated. Nevertheless, in the medium to long term significant growth in demand must be expected and nuclear power is likely to figure prominently in capacity expansion plans.

Other non-OPEC developing countries

This group of countries, by definition, includes all those WOCA nations which have not been considered thus far. Of the 120 countries which fall into this category, a very large number have no current nuclear plans and will not be considering nuclear power as a viable option for the foreseeable future (for example Vanuatu, Kiribati and East Timor may all confidently be classified as non-nuclear nations). The following are considered to be among the most likely candidates for nuclear power within the timescale considered in this chapter.

Israel
Syria
Turkey
Hong Kong
Singapore
Papua New Guinea
Pakistan
Other Latin American countries

Of these, Pakistan has one small reactor and plans to build a second of 600–900 MW capacity; Chile, Peru and Colombia along with some of the other countries in Latin America could have some nuclear power by the end of the century; Israel has the potential to construct 1–2 GW by 2000 but may be constrained for reasons of national security; Turkey is considering the option of installing one or two nuclear units in the 600–900 MW range for service in the late 1990s. Nuclear capacity to 1990 will be negligible and even by 2000 is likely to be small, given the weak market in which reactor vendors are currently operating. Beyond the end of the century nuclear growth is possible but small grid sizes will remain a severe obstacle to nuclear expansion in many countries well beyond the year 2000.

Other non-OPEC developing countries nuclear capacity (GW)	
1978	0
1982	0
1985	0
1990	0
2000	2–7

3

The frequency of core meltdown accidents

A core meltdown at a nuclear reactor is arguably the most worrying risk associated with energy production and conversion. Such an accident could occur in a light water reactor (LWR) if some failure of the reactor coolant supply caused the core to be partially or wholly uncovered, and led to fuel element temperatures in excess of the melting point of the cladding or even the uranium dioxide fuel itself.

In such a loss of coolant accident, it is likely that the neutron chain reaction would be rapidly curtailed by the insertion of control rods or some other neutron absorbing medium such as borated water. However, the substantial residual heat generated within the fuel by the decay of fission products may amount to 15 MW, 24 hours after shutdown of a 1200 MW(e) LWR. Failure to remove this heat will result in a partial or complete core meltdown.

For a meltdown to lead to a serious accident, the reactor containment building must also be breached. The consequences of this could be a major release of radioactivity, contaminating several hundred square miles and possibly causing thousands of casualties.[1] Such a sequence of events will occur infrequently, but not so rarely that the possibility of core meltdowns may safely be dismissed.[2]

In this chapter we examine various ways of calculating the frequency with which nuclear core meltdowns will occur in the future. In other energy industries, such as coal mining, current views on future accident rates are heavily influenced by the wealth of experience of past accidents, modified by the application of judgement and changing perceptions. We apply the same two elements, operating experience and judgement, to calculate nuclear reactor core meltdown frequencies. The results of these calculations justify the wording of the first sentence of this chapter; the risks from coal mining accidents may be numerically greater, but the uncertainties in what we know of the risks of a core meltdown quite justifiably cause more anxiety.

Table 3.1 *Deaths due to accidents*
at US coal mines 1966–9

Year	Deaths per million tons of coal output
1966	0.43
1967	0.40
1968	0.56
1969	0.36

Coal mining accidents

Experience

Our experience of mining and using coal is vast and in the UK is documented as far back as the twelfth century.[3] So too is our experience of the risks from these activities. For much of its history, coal mining has been a dirty and exceedingly dangerous business, and although 'it goes without saying that conditions of mining have improved immeasurably over the years . . . the past legacy of dirt and danger often accompanied by harsh struggles cannot be overestimated'.[4]

Nowadays much of the risk associated with the extraction and use of coal comes from chronic illnesses which claim lives every year: lung diseases such as pneumoconiosis amongst miners brought on by the inhalation of coal dust, and bronchitis aggravated by the airborne products of coal combustion in industrial areas. However, mine accidents also exact a regular toll of lives each year, when viewed across the whole industry.

Table 3.1 shows accident deaths among American coal miners in the late 1960s.[5] The figures in this table have been adjusted to remove the effect of varying output and are shown as deaths per million tons of coal produced. Although the casualties fluctuate from year to year they lie within a small enough range that it seems quite proper to apply an averaging process and talk about the mean number of accidental deaths per unit of output being 0.44 per million tons in American mines from 1966 to 1969.[6] Going further, it does not seem unreasonable to view the actual figures for 1966 to 1969 as a sample of four from a hypothetical infinite population of possible values that could have been obtained. It is possible to calculate, using the sample standard deviation of 0.09 deaths per million tons, just how closely we might expect the mean number of deaths per unit of output to resemble the figure we actually obtained if we could somehow wipe the slate clean and go back and experience the years 1966 to 1969 for a second time. We find that we could be 95% sure that

Table 3.2 *Deaths due to accidents at US coal mines 1951–70*

Period	Deaths per year	Output per year (million tons)	Deaths per million tons of coal output
1951–5	522	449	1.16
1956–60	380	424	0.90
1961–5	274	428	0.64
1966–70	246	515	0.48

the mean value would be within 0.14 of our sample mean of 0.44 deaths per million tons.[7] However, from the point of view of policy analysis, the important question would be this: Suppose we had been considering starting a new mine in the United States in 1970. Would we have been justified in using these results to say that we would be 95% sure that the mean number of accident fatalities from our mine over its lifetime would be between 0.30 and 0.58 deaths per million tons of coal mined? The answer to this policy question is no. And the reason is that even with such a long-established and statistically rich activity as coal mining, the results of experience must be combined with judgement and changing perceptions if we wish to say anything about the future.

Judgement

Firstly, the risks from coal mining have been changing with time. Extending the series in table 3.1 backwards in time gives the fatalities shown in table 3.2; deaths per unit of output in the USA have been steadily declining.[8] To ignore this information would probably lead to overestimation of risks in the future.

Secondly, the figures in tables 3.1 and 3.2 refer to all mines, both old and new. If better standards of safety occur partly through improved methods that can only be introduced at the start of a mine's life, then newer mines will always tend to be safer than the average. Ignoring this information would also lead to overestimation of risks for a new mine to be started in 1970.

Thirdly, exhaustible resource theory indicates that the best deposits of a mineral such as coal should be exploited first.[9] The lower-grade reserves that remain to be tapped by new mines could well be more dangerous as well as more costly. On the other hand, if increased pressure on energy supplies leads to greater exploration, some of the new fields discovered are likely to be of better than average quality and safety.

To extend this point, physical characteristics, methods of working, and the experience of the miners all play a part in determining the risk from a new mine. Since each new mine, each new face, each new shift is unique, there will never be a completely appropriate statistical series from which a totally objective estimate of the level of risk in a new mine can be obtained.

While the time trend of risks in coal mining can perhaps be modelled using a regression analysis (requiring judgement only in the choice of explanatory variables and the form of function to be fitted), as we move down our list of qualifications we encounter factors whose importance can only be estimated by using our knowledge of the particular mine to modify the mean value of deaths per unit output in the coal industry as a whole. Exercising this judgement will often reduce our estimate of the risks in the case of coal. For instance, the members of the UK Commission on Energy and the Environment described their frame of mind at the start of their study, *Coal and the Environment*: 'Our initial expectation was that vigorous examination of the environmental impact of coal production, use and conversion would inevitably throw up a picture highlighting their deleterious effects.' Despite this, the members felt able to conclude that 'there are no insuperable environmental obstacles to the role of coal as currently envisaged in the UK . . . we have indicated areas where higher standards may be needed. We consider that these can be achieved.' In other words, they estimated future environmental impacts by applying their judgement to the lessons of experience and concluded that these amended impacts would be acceptable.

Most observers would therefore agree that judgement as well as experience must be used when thinking about future risks from mining and using coal. We now wish to assert that the same holds true for nuclear power. To date, judgement, albeit highly quantified, has played the major role in the assessment of the risks from nuclear power. But actual operating experience of nuclear stations also has a tale to tell, one that will become increasingly important as the amount of electricity generated by nuclear power increases. Let us now examine what each of these two methods tells us about the future risks of nuclear core meltdowns.

LWR core meltdowns

Experience
Mankind has had only 25 years experience of operating commercial nuclear power stations. For most of this quarter century the rates of operation have been low. In the year 1960, less than half of a giga-watt year (GWyr) of nuclear electricity was generated worldwide. By 1970 this had risen to nearly 9 GWyr,[10] and in 1980 over 70 GWyr of electricity was

Table 3.3 *Worldwide LWR core meltdowns and operating experience*

Period	Core meltdowns	Reactor years	Cumulative reactor years
pre-1970	0	100	100
1971–5	0	250	350
1976	0	51	401
1977	0	59	460
1978	0	69	529
1979	1	70	599
1980	0	75	674
1981	0	88	762
1982	0	96	858

nuclear generated.[11] By the end of 1980 the cumulative total of nuclear-generated electricity worldwide was approaching 500 GWyr. On the other hand, fossil-fuelled power stations have generated over 500 GWyr of electricity in each year since the early 1970s.

Different types of nuclear reactor have very different operating characteristics and there is little reason to suppose that their susceptibility to core meltdown is identical. However, the major part of the operating experience with nuclear power comes from the operation of LWRs. In 1981, they generated 73 GWyr, or 88% of the WOCAs nuclear total of 82 GWyr.[12] Differences exist between LWRs, such as the differences between PWRs and BWRs, between PWRs supplied by different manufacturers, and even between PWRs from the same supplier but of differing size and vintage. Nevertheless, all power reactors within a given country are generally required to meet the same standards of safety, and differences in standards between countries are being reduced as licensing arrangements and exchange-of-information agreements become the order of the day. In addition, all LWRs share strong generic similarities. For these reasons we believe that it is not unreasonable to use LWR operating experience to evaluate limits on the frequency of LWR core meltdowns.

Table 3.3 gives the data that enable us to do this. It shows our operating experience of LWRs to date and the number of core meltdowns in each year. There are three possible ways of expressing the increase in nuclear operating experience during a year, none of which are entirely satisfactory: the number of GWyr of nuclear-generated electricity; the number of reactor years, counting each reactor as one whether it operated for 10% or 90% of the time; the number of reactor years, weighting each reactor by its load factor during the year. We choose the third of these. There is no reason to believe that a 1 GW reactor is any more likely to melt down than a 250 MW reactor, since the control systems on all power reactors are very similar. We exclude very small and research reactors from our database, since their control systems do differ from those in the larger power reactors with which we are mainly concerned.[13] Since a meltdown is extremely unlikely to occur at a shutdown reactor,[14] we count a reactor operating at a 50% annual average load factor as 0.5 reactor years and so on.

In many ways table 3.3 is analogous to table 3.2 presenting coal mining accident data. The main difference is the rarity of core meltdowns, both absolutely and in comparison with the frequency of accidents at mines. The entry for 1979 is the accident at Three Mile Island (TMI) in Pennsylvania. At the time of writing, four years after the accident, it is still not certain that the damage to the core of the reactor is serious enough to warrant a 1 rather than a zero in the table.[15] However, the very high likelihood of at least partial melting makes an entry of 1 more reasonable than zero. The chapter conclusions would not be weakened if the 1 were replaced by, say, 0.5 to reflect this ignorance.

In Chapter 1 we tried to recapture the optimism concerning the economics and relative safety of nuclear power that existed amongst the technical community in the late 1970s. What would an observer at that time, in 1978 for example, have made of the experience of LWR safety

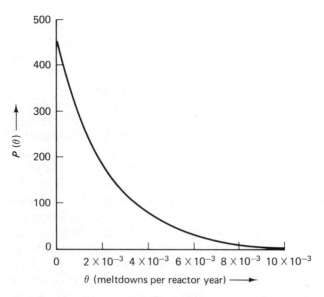

Figure 3.1 The frequency of core meltdowns: operating experience to end 1977

presented in table 3.3? Assuming no clairvoyance, only the figures to the end of 1977 would have been visible, indicating a total of no core meltdowns in 460 reactor years of LWR operation up to that date.

This experience would have allowed some conclusions to be drawn about the underlying frequency of core meltdowns in light water reactors; for example, that it was very unlikely to be as high as one every ten reactor years. Figure 3.1 shows the full extent of the conclusions that could have been drawn from aggregate operating experience to the end of 1977.[16] The horizontal axis measures the frequency of LWR core meltdowns per reactor year. The vertical axis measures how likely any particular frequency is, given the operating experience of 460 reactor years. This figure and figure 3.2 are in the form of probability density functions. The probability that the frequency is between θ_1 and θ_2 meltdowns per reactor year is given by the area under the curve between θ_1 and θ_2. So, for example, in figure 3.1 the probability that the frequency lies between 4×10^{-3} and 6×10^{-3} meltdowns per reactor year is about $[30 + 0.5(70 - 30)] \times 2 \times 10^{-3}$. This works out at 0.10, or 10%. The calculation is essentially the same as the one we performed earlier in this chapter for the risks from coal mining accidents.[17]

Figure 3.1 shows that at the end of 1977 the most likely value for the frequency of core meltdowns was zero, as might have been expected with none having occurred up to that date. Our observer could also have concluded, as we suspected, that the probability of the frequency being 0.1 per reactor year or higher was small; so small that it does not even show up on the figure. In fact, operating experience to the end of 1977 practically ruled out all values for the frequency of core meltdowns higher than about 6.5×10^{-3} per reactor year, or one every 154 reactor years. If

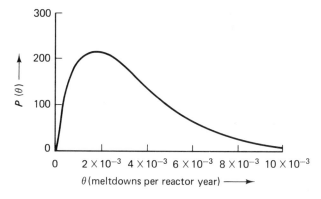

Figure 3.2 The frequency of core meltdowns: operating experience to end 1979

the frequency had been as high as this, we would have expected to see three meltdowns in the 460 reactor years of operation to the end of 1977. The actual experience of no core meltdowns gave only a 5% chance that the frequency was as high as this.[18]

Then TMI occurred. If we count this accident as a core meltdown, the lesson of the operating record at the end of 1979 became that shown in figure 3.2.[19] The most likely frequency of core meltdowns had moved upwards from zero to 1.67×10^{-3} per reactor year, or one in 600 years of operation. The experience of TMI meant that if we had been forced to pick a single figure to express the frequency of core meltdowns at the end of 1979 we would no longer have chosen such a low figure as at the end of 1977.

The highest core meltdown frequency compatible with the aggregate operating record had also increased at the end of 1979 to 7.9×10^{-3} per reactor year, or once in 126 reactor years. With this frequency, we would have expected 4.75 core meltdowns to have occurred by the end of 1979. The actual experience of a single meltdown gave only a 5% chance that the frequency was as high as this.[20] The 95% upper limit had passed this value on its way down in 1976, when cumulative experience reached 380 reactor years with no meltdowns. It must have been a great disappointment to nuclear proponents to see it increase once again. However, in contrast to the best estimate, the effect of TMI on the upper limit was comparatively modest. This is because the second role of extra experience is to make us more confident that the true meltdown frequency is somewhere close to the value we have observed. It is just as surprising to have observed only one meltdown when 4.75 were expected as it is to have observed none when three were expected.

At the end of 1979 this confidence-inspiring process had not gone very far. Even by the end of 1982, with cumulative experience at 858 reactor years, the range of possible core meltdown frequencies is still fairly wide, with a 90% chance of lying between 4.1×10^{-4} and 5.6×10^{-3} per reactor year.[21] But as more and more electricity is generated in LWR reactors, this aspect of extra experience will gain in importance. Even on our pessimistic view presented in Chapter 2, worldwide experience with LWRs will have exceeded 1600 reactor years by 1990 and 3000 reactor years by 2000.[22] The debate over the safety in operation of nuclear power may well be over one way or the other by the end of the century; protagonists will be able to make their points with some force by appealing to an operating record almost 4 times richer than is available today. At the very least, the position of nuclear power will be recognised as similar to coal mining at present where arguments over safety in operation are settled by reference to experience tempered with judgement. We have not yet reached that position; with our limited experience of nuclear power, the debate over nuclear safety has so far been conducted almost entirely by appeals to judgement. Let us see how that judgement has been changing over the years.

Judgement

We mentioned some of the caveats about using accident frequencies from the statistical record to make policy decisions when we discussed the safety of coal mining. All the same problems of non-stationarity, vintage effects and uniqueness will require the use of judgement in the interpretation of accident statistics for nuclear power. Indeed the process has already started. Observers suggest that future nuclear power stations will be safer than those of today as a result of the lessons learned at the TMI accident.[23] The implication is that the frequency of core meltdowns will be lower in the future and so the estimates we derived above from operating experience are not appropriate. Instead, the majority of judgements concerning nuclear power safety to date have ignored the aggregate operating record in favour of a divide and conquer technique known as probabilistic risk assessment (PRA).

Any PRA is centred around three basic questions. (i) What can go wrong? (ii) How likely is it that this will happen? (iii) If it happens what are the consequences? These questions are asked of the multitude of events, such as a valve failing to operate correctly, that might be expected to occur in such a complex plant as a nuclear power station. The answers to questions (i) and (iii) show that some sequences of events lead to core meltdowns. The answers to question (ii) are combined to give an estimate of the likelihood of occurrence of each sequence. The frequency of a core meltdown is then judged to be the sum of the frequencies of all the separate sequences that lead to this outcome.[24]

The first large-scale application of PRA to civilian nuclear power was WASH-1400, published in 1975 by the US Nuclear Regulatory Commission.[25] The judgement of the WASH-1400 PRA was that the frequency of core meltdowns in the two American LWR reactors studied had a 50% chance of being less than 5×10^{-5} per reactor year (once every 20,000 reactor years), and a 95% chance of being less than 3×10^{-4} per reactor year (once every 3333 reactor years). Although some misgivings were expressed about the executive summary, the main body of WASH-1400 was generally viewed as a praiseworthy attempt at a difficult calculation.[26] The main criticism of substance was that some of the procedures used to evaluate the frequency of core meltdown would tend to understate the uncertainty in the final result.[27] So the general judgement of critics was that while the median frequency of WASH-1400 was probably about right, the upper limit should probably be increased by some unspecified amount.

This was the state of the art in 1978. People had little trouble recon-
ciling the stories told by experience and judgement. The median frequency of WASH-1400 was close enough to zero to have been expected to
produce no core melts to date, and that is indeed what had been observed.
The upper limit estimate of WASH-1400, one meltdown every 3333
reactor years, especially when adjusted to allow for the underestimation
of uncertainty, was perhaps an order of magnitude lower than the upper
limit derived from experience, but of course that was why a PRA was
needed in the first place, because the upper limit deducible from experience was so lax. Obvious inconsistencies between experience and judgement were absent.

The use of PRAs to form judgements about nuclear power safety has
increased greatly since 1978. Thirteen major studies of individual nuclear
plants in the USA have been initiated since the accident at TMI.[28] Results
from these studies are now beginning to be published. One of the first to
be released, in late 1981, was for the Zion Station operated and analysed
by Commonwealth Edison.[29] This reactor was singled out for attention
because it was initially thought that Zion might represent an undue share
of the risk from nuclear reactors in the USA because of its proximity to
areas of high population density. The results of the PRA were reassuring.
Far from presenting an undue risk, the median estimate of the early
fatalities from the Zion station was found to be about three orders of
magnitude below the values calculated in WASH-1400. For instance, the
median estimate of the frequency of an event that would cause 100 early
fatalities was just slightly over 10^{-10} per reactor year, or once in ten
billion reactor years of operation. The uncertainties were judged to be
such that the authors were 90% confident that the frequency of such an
event would be less than 4×10^{-9} per reactor year, or once every 250
million reactor years.[30]

The differences between the WASH-1400 and Zion figures came largely
from a different treatment of the various possible outcomes following
a core meltdown. Thus the Zion median estimate of core meltdown,
4.42×10^{-5} per reactor year is only slightly lower than the WASH-1400
median estimate of 5×10^{-5} per reactor year. However, since the Zion
PRA is claimed to represent a significant advance in the state of the art in
risk assessment of nuclear power plants, the authors clearly believe that
their results are not subject to the charges concerning the inadequate
treatment of uncertainty that bedevilled WASH-1400.

Now compare the Zion PRA results with the lesson of experience. The
Zion study says that the median estimate of the frequency of core
meltdowns is once every 23,000 reactor years. There is no compelling
reason to believe that the Zion station is any more or less safe than the

typical LWR operating during the 1970s. The aggregate operating record to end-1982 gives a most likely value for frequency of core meltdowns in these reactors of once every 858 reactor years. The gulf between these figures remains even if we examine ranges instead of best estimates. Aggregate operating experience proclaims there is a 95% chance that the frequency is more than once every 2450 reactor years, and that there is only a 0.07% chance that the frequency is as low as the Zion median estimate.[31] Is it any wonder if informed observers begin to feel uneasy? The output of PRAs and the testimony of aggregate operating experience appear irreconcilable.

In this analysis of LWR experience so far, we have used a very coarse sieve to sort events into just the two categories of 'meltdown' or 'no meltdown'. Despite only catching one event in our sieve we have been able to draw some conclusions about underlying frequencies. What happens if we use a finer mesh and look at precursors to meltdowns as well as meltdowns themselves? The answer is that nothing much changes. A recent Oak Ridge study that looked at 169 meltdown precursors occurring from 1969 to 1979 concluded that the best estimate for the frequency of meltdown during that decade is 1 in 500 reactor years, strikingly similar to our best estimate of 1 in 600 reactor years at the end of 1979. Even removing TMI from the Oak Ridge data base only changes the best estimate to 1 in 1500 reactor years.[32] The PRA results still look worryingly out of line with both the aggregate and disaggregate operating record.

The conflict between judgement and experience

Earlier we pointed out that some nuclear proponents would play down the importance of this discrepancy when making policy decisions about the future of nuclear power. Their reason would be that the latest reactor designs are significantly different from those that make up the bulk of the operating record. The CEGB's estimate of core meltdown frequency in its planned Sizewell B PWR is 1.16×10^{-6} per reactor year, or one meltdown every 860,000 reactor years.[33] This is fully 1000 times safer than the median meltdown frequency derived from operating experience of light water reactors to date. Such an improvement in safety would truly make the message of experience irrelevant.

Can the passage of a few years and the lessons learned from the accident at TMI really have made the nuclear reactors now under construction that much safer than those making up the bulk of the operating record? Several pointers indicate that it would be wise to be sceptical.

To accept the judgement of PRAs above the lessons of experience, it is essential that the PRA analysts be infallible in one respect: they must have thought of everything that could possibly go wrong in a nuclear power station. Both anecdotal and research evidence suggests they have not. Casual observation of the inappropriate responses by fallible operators in nuclear and other power plants provides the anecdotal evidence. The Browns Ferry operator who disabled the emergency core-cooling system by setting fire to cables under the control room with a candle while searching for an air leak is the classic example, but many others exist. It is hard to believe that all such possible bizarre responses have been captured in the PRA studies.

This scepticism is strengthened by research results which show the inability of even expert subjects to appreciate just how incomplete the PRA-type analyses are. For example, skilled automobile engineers were told that a car had failed to start and asked to assign probabilities to various causes such as a fault in the battery, the fuel system, ignition system and so on. One of the causes was a catch-all 'other' category, and it was discovered that even when quite major problems such as the ignition system fault were 'pruned' from the 'tree' and not mentioned explicitly, the probability assigned to the category 'other' rose far less than it should.[34] If recognising analytical in-completeness is difficult for even such a well-understood and simple system as a car engine, how much harder must it be for a nuclear reactor? One critic summarises the technical problem concisely: 'Nuclear power systems are so complex that the probability the safety analysis contains serious errors is so big as to render meaningless the tiny computed probability of accident.'[35]

Psychological studies have also shown that professionals and laymen alike tend to be overconfident of their ability to make judgements about probabilities. Typically, events that are claimed to have only a 10% chance of occurring turn out to be true 30% of the time, and an assessed proba-bility of 1% corresponds to an actual probability of 20%.[36] The insistence of nuclear proponents that no major failure modes could possibly have been omitted from the latest studies[37] is no guarantee that in fact none have been.

So the core meltdown frequencies predicted by experience and judge-ment remain in conflict. The sophisticated form of averaging known as Bayesian statistics can be employed to gloss over the conflict and produce a best estimate for the meltdown frequency from experience and judgement combined.[38] But this is not really much comfort, because it requires belief in the judgement implicit in the PRAs. Instead, suspension of disbelief is one of the first casualties of the conflict between judgement and experience since 1978. People remember the reassuring estimates of reactor safety made before TMI and feel that if the experts were wrong before, they can be wrong again.

The impact of future experience

As time goes by and more nuclear electricity is generated, the story told by operating experience will once again come more into line with the meltdown frequencies predicted by the PRAs, provided no more core meltdowns occur. The WASH-1400 PRA, for example, gives a 95% probability that the meltdown frequency is less than 3×10^{-4} per reactor year. If no more occur, the 5% lower limit from operating experience will drop to this level from its end-1982 value of 4.1×10^{-4} per reactor year when 1170 reactor years of experience have been gained. Even on our low projections of Chapter 2 this will occur by 1985. By this time it will at least be possible to say that the error bars around the estimates of judgement and experience overlap, although the most likely estimates of experience and the median estimate of the WASH-1400 PRA will not coincide until 20,000 reactor years have passed. This will not occur until well after the turn of the century.

The future will not be so reassuring if another core meltdown occurs. If this should happen, the 95% upper limit, the most likely estimate, and the 5% lower limit meltdown frequency estimates will immediately increase by factors of 1.3, 2.0 and 2.3 respectively.[39] The very modest increase in the upper limit is a reflection of the second role of extra experience; increasing confidence that the true frequency is close to what has been observed. Unfortunately the large increase in the lower limit is the reverse of the coin. If another core meltdown does occur, the lower limit from experience will not drop back to 3×10^{-4} per reactor year until 2730 reactor years of experience have been gained. On our projections this will not occur before 1995. In the meantime, if the second core meltdown occurred in, say, 1985 after 1200 reactor years of operation, it would be impossible to sustain the argument that the PRA-based results of WASH-1400, let alone the more optimistic results produced more recently, are even roughly correct. We consider, in Chapter 5, how the possibility of future accidents should affect the choice of nuclear reactor, and, in Chapter 9, how a final loss of faith in PRA results might form a barrier to trade in nuclear electricity.

4

Hidden costs of the accident at Three Mile Island

The worst accident to have occurred to date at a civil nuclear power station, and one which had a profound effect on the nuclear community world-wide, took place on 28 March 1979 at the Three Mile Island Unit 2 reactor (TMI-2) in Pennsylvania, USA. Coming as it did at a time when nuclear capital costs were continuing to show significant increases in real terms,[1,2] and lead-times were lengthening beyond the planning horizons employed by most utilities, the timing of the accident was particularly inopportune. The accident also served to heighten the growing public concern over reactor safety and has changed perceptions regarding accident frequencies, as discussed in the previous chapter. It also did nothing to reduce the extraordinarily long licensing process experienced in countries such as the US and West Germany during the late 1970s and early 1980s.

The accident itself, which is fully documented in the report of the President's Commission,[3] was, from the point of view of injury to operating staff and adverse physical health effects to the general public, relatively minor (emissions of radioactivity, for example, being far lower than those estimated for the Windscale fire in the UK in 1957).[4] The reason why TMI has assumed such obvious importance is because this was the first major accident at a modern, commercial-sized nuclear power plant, and it revealed many shortcomings and failings by personnel and institutions within the nuclear industry. That the accident can seriously be regarded as major when no directly attributable loss of life is ever likely to be apparent may be explained by considering the costs of the accident, both direct and indirect, some of which are listed below:

(1) The direct cost of the clean-up operation at TMI-2 is estimated to be between \$975 and \$1034 million,[5,6] figures which do not include provision for either decommissioning or reconstructing the stricken reactor. This is an unavoidable cost which must be met in order to bring the reactor into a safe and stable condition, a situation which

will not now be reached before mid-1988. (The end of clean-up is defined as the return of the plant to a radiological condition typical of normal operating plants.)

(2) The cost of writing off what was essentially a new reactor (the total cumulative gross generation figure of 2126 GWh for TMI-2 is equivalent to 3 months full power operation, the accident taking place just one year after initial criticality). Current estimates of nuclear capital costs would put the figure involved somewhere in the range of $1000–3000 million. For the full cost to be attributed to the accident, it is necessary to assume that TMI-2 will never again be operated as a commercial nuclear power station and that no scrap or recovery value should be assigned to the plant. While the former is almost certain to be true, given the extent of damage to the plant, the second assumption is probably over-pessimistic and some reduction to the capital cost figure should be made.

(3) Marginal costs of replacement generation have to be met by the owners of TMI-2. These costs, which will ultimately be borne by consumers, are likely to be significant, particularly as it was considered necessary to shut down TMI-1 immediately following the accident. The undamaged TMI-1 plant remains non-operational four years after the accident.

(4) The effect of the TMI accident has been to lower confidence generally in the nuclear industry, costs being associated with such an erosion of confidence for a number of reasons. For example, additional post-TMI regulatory requirements have led to increased construction times for stations currently being built. Such delays lead to increased costs principally through higher interest charges. Another possible cost component would be the higher tenders necessarily produced by nuclear steam supply system (NSSS) manufacturers in a highly depressed market although it would be unreasonable to attribute the current low rate of nuclear ordering solely to TMI (the poor performance of most Western economies and corresponding downturn of electricity demand in recent years being an obviously important factor as discussed in Chapter 2).

(5) There is another cost which may conceivably be laid at the door of TMI. If, in the period immediately after the accident, nuclear utilities worldwide adopted a cautious approach and either shut down or de-rated reactors while investigations were made as to whether a similar accident might occur at their plant, then the costs of such action in terms of replacement generation costs may be appreciable when summed over a large number of reactors.

In this chapter we are concerned with this last possible effect and, in the following analysis, show that such an effect was indeed observed.[7]

Effect of TMI on reactor load factors

Worldwide

One of the ways of determining what effect, if any, the TMI accident had on the output of nuclear power stations worldwide is by performing a systematic study of power station load factors. The load factor of a nuclear station is here defined as the ratio of electricity generated in a given period to the amount that would have been generated had the station operated at full design output throughout the period. By comparing the load factors of a large number of nuclear stations in the period before 28 March 1979, with the load factors achieved following the accident, it is possible to determine whether a general drop in load factor occurred and, if so, for how long it persisted.

The data necessary for such a study come from a quarterly compilation in the nuclear industry trade journal *Nuclear Engineering International*.[8] In this review, moving annual load factors are given for all nuclear power stations in the Western world having reactors of 150 MW gross design electrical output and above. All load factors relate gross electrical generation to gross design output capacity. In addition, figures are provided for cumulative lifetime generation at the end of each quarter from which average three-monthly load factors may be obtained for each station. Rather than average these three-monthly load factors for nuclear stations appearing in the review, we produce separate averages for each of the four main commercial reactor types suitably weighted by reactor design output. In this way, weighted three-monthly load factors are obtained for all PWRs, BWRs, PHWRs (principally Candu reactors, but also included is the Argentinian Atucha 1 heavy water reactor), and Magnox reactors covered by the review. We omit the TMI-2 reactor from the analysis because the purpose of this chapter is to determine the effect of a major nuclear accident on other nuclear stations; we have already assumed that TMI-2 will not generate electricity again in the future.

The resulting load factors are shown in figure 4.1. Before attempting to analyse these results in detail, two general observations may be made. Firstly, the PHWR (Candu) reactor appears to be the best performer, as is indicated by the consistently high load factors achieved. Secondly, the Magnox reactors are generally poor performers, which exhibit a particularly strong seasonal component in their three-monthly load factors. This generally poor performance may be attributed to the systematic downrating on almost all Magnox reactors, which has been necessary to reduce steel oxidation. The large seasonal component is due to extended outages during the summer (low demand) months. These outages, required under statutory regulations, result in one of the two reactors at each station being unavailable for between six and fifteen weeks during the summer.

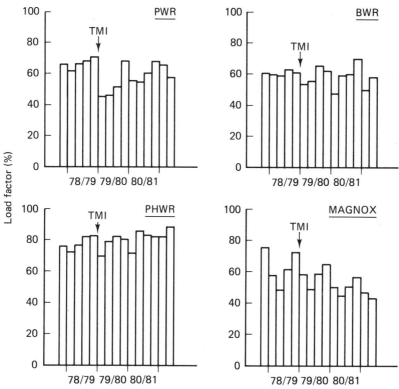

Figure 4.1 Quarterly load factors for principal reactor types (non-Communist world)

From figure 4.1, it may be seen that there is evidence of a reduction in load factors of PWRs immediately following the TMI accident, followed by a subsequent gradual recovery. For PHWRs and BWRs, a fall is also observed in the three-monthly load factor following the accident but care must be exercised here as this drop coincides with a seasonal load factor reduction. In order to determine whether a real post-TMI response occurred, we perform a paired t statistic test on the four pairs of quarterly load factor values appearing in each of the periods: April 1978–March 1979 (1978/9) and April 1979–March 1980 (1979/80). Similar tests are performed for the periods 1979/80 and 1980/81 and also 1978/79 and 1980/81. In this

Table 4.1 *Load factor analysis for principal reactor types
(non-communist world)*

	Percentage mean annual load factor (Total mid-year capacity–GW)			Paired *t* statistics on quarterly load factors		
	78/79*	79/80	80/81	78/79– 79/80	79/80– 80/81	78/79– 80/81
PWR	66.8 (44.3)	53.1 (53.4)	60.0 (59.5)	3.54	−2.93	3.66
BWR	61.2 (27.4)	59.7 (33.1)	59.9 (37.1)	0.75	−0.06	0.29
PHWR	78.4 (4.6)	78.0 (5.3)	80.8 (6.3)	0.36	−2.06	−1.14
MAGNOX	60.3 (8.5)	57.9 (8.5)	50.9 (8.5)	1.23	7.00	3.67

* Financial years from 1 April to 31 March are used throughout this report. The TMI accident occurred on 28 March 1979. 78/79 can be considered to represent the twelve-month period prior to the accident and 79/80 the twelve months immediately following the accident.

way, the performance of each reactor type for the year prior to the accident is compared with the performance for the two years following the accident so that seasonal effects are removed. The results of this analysis are shown in table 4.1 which also gives average annual load factor figures.

The tentative conclusions that we have drawn from figure 4.1 are reinforced by the statistical analysis presented in table 4.1. The average annual load factor for PWRs falls from 66.8% prior to the accident to 53.1% after the accident. The *t* statistic of 3.54 for PWRs shows that the difference in quarterly load factors in the twelve-month periods before and after the accident is significant at the 97.5% level for a one-tailed test with three degrees of freedom. The other reactor types do not show differences significant at the 90% level.

The importance of this drop in PWR load factors is amplified by the gross capacity figures for each reactor type which are also given in table 4.1. In September 1979, the capacity of PWRs was over 20 GW more than BWRs, the next most common reactor type. In addition, all data in table 4.1 (and figure 4.1) refer to commercial reactors of 150 MW gross and above, which have been operational for at least one year. In this way distortions produced by reactors having low load factors in their first year of operation, a problem which occurs at most new power stations, should have been eliminated. To verify that this in fact was the case and that the fall in load factor after March 1979 was not simply due to the 9.1 GW of new nuclear plant (an increase from 44.3 GW in mid-1978 to 53.4 GW in mid-1979) performing badly, we investigate separately the additional stations included in the analysis between September 1978 and September 1979. This reveals that the new stations were not systematically poor performers, many of them (in particular some of the French PWRs) having remarkably high load factors for stations which had been operating for this relatively short time.

The fact that PWRs exhibited such a large load factor reduction in the year after TMI, when no corresponding fall was observed in BWRs in particular, is noteworthy for a number of reasons. Both PWRs and BWRs represent US reactor systems which are similar in many ways (both employ light water as moderator and coolant, for example). Also, more than half the PWRs and BWRs in the Western world in mid-1979 were operating in the US and were thus subject to the same regulatory control. For this reason, it might have been supposed that BWRs would show some post-TMI load factor reduction from which the Canadian PHWR and British Magnox reactors might have been immune. The data in table 4.1 indicate that this is not the case and there is no evidence to suggest that worldwide BWR performance suffered as a result of the accident.

It is also possible to see from table 4.1 the extent to which PWR load factors recovered following the initial fall. In the second year after the accident, the average annual load factor was 60%, an improvement of 6.9 percentage points over the previous year. The paired t statistic figures indicate that the improvement in three-monthly load factors from 1979/80 to 1980/81 was significant at the 95% level ($t = -2.93$). Even with this improvement the average PWR load factor in the second year after the accident was still 6.8 percentage points lower than the average load factor before the accident and the t statistic of 3.66 between the 1978/79 and 1980/81 three-monthly load factors is highly significant.[9] It therefore appears that PWR performance in the Western world (as measured by load factor) fell sharply in the year immediately after TMI but showed signs of recovery in the second year after the accident. Two years after the accident, however, this recovery was not complete. Data to March 1982 (1981/82 twelve-month load factor 61%) indicate that pre-accident performance levels were also not achieved in the third year after TMI.

We have shown that TMI had little effect on the performance of BWRs worldwide and the effect, if any, on PHWRs was likewise insignificant. Some explanation is, however, required for the Magnox figures presented in table 4.1. Although there is some evidence to suggest that Magnox load factors fell in the year following TMI, a larger, and statistically much

Table 4.2 *Load factor analysis for US PWRs and BWRs*

| | Percentage mean annual load factor (Total mid-year capacity–GW) | | | Paired t statistics on quarterly load factors | | |
	78/79	79/80	80/81	78/79–79/80	79/80–80/81	78/79–80/81
PWR	65.7 (29.2)	49.1 (33.1)	56.2 (33.8)	3.99	−1.91	2.47
BWR	66.1 (17.6)	62.5 (18.5)	61.1 (18.5)	1.00	0.22	1.64

more significant, reduction in load factor occurred in the second year after the accident. This overall decline of Magnox load factors with time is due to extended outages which began in the first quarter of 1980 at two stations, Dungeness A and Bradwell. These outages, which were necessary to remedy welding defects found in the gas circuit, have no connection with TMI but have had a significant effect on overall Magnox performance because of the small sample size of just 8.5 GW.

United States

Having identified a significant fall in worldwide PWR load factors following TMI, we repeat the above analysis for US reactors only. In this way, we are able to determine whether the worldwide effect represents a strong US reaction moderated to a certain degree by PWRs operating in other countries, or whether a genuine international response to the accident was made. In addition, we thought it possible that US BWR load factors might show some post-TMI effect which was not evident when all BWRs in the Western world were considered.

The basis for the analysis is similar to that used above. The database consists of US PWRs and BWRs of 150 MW gross and above which have operated for at least one year (TMI-2 again being excluded). The average three-monthly load factors are shown in figure 4.2 and average annual load factors, along with paired t statistics, are given in table 4.2.

The results for the US are broadly in line with the results for PWRs and BWRs worldwide. The fall in average annual load factor for US PWRs in the year following TMI is 16.6 percentage points, the t statistic for three-monthly load factors for the twelve months before and after the accident being highly significant ($t = 3.99$). This compares with a fall of 13.7 percentage points for all PWRs and, when account is taken of the proportion of PWRs which are operating in the US, indicates that a significant

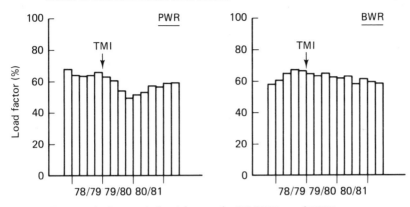

Figure 4.2 Quarterly load factors for US PWRs and BWRs

load factor reduction (8.7 percentage points) may be attributed to non-US reactors. In other words, while a somewhat greater deterioration in performance of US PWRs is apparent, the effect of the TMI accident on PWR load factors worldwide has been marked. The inclusion in the US PWR database of the TMI-1 reactor does not account for the sharp fall in load factor following the accident. Indeed, if it is omitted, along with TMI-2, a reduction of 15.3 percentage points in the US annual average PWR load factor in the year after TMI is still observed.

The extent to which recovery in performance of US PWRs has taken place is similar to that for all PWRs. An improvement of 7.1 percentage points was observed in the average annual US load factor in the second year after the accident but, once again, it is apparent that the recovery, as reflected by annual load factor, was not complete by the end of the second year.

Table 4.2 offers some evidence of a BWR load factor reduction post-TMI. In the twelve months after the accident the average load factor of BWRs was 3.6 percentage points lower than during the previous twelve months. However, a comparison of three-monthly load factors before and after the accident indicates that differences are not significant at the 90% level. For this reason, we conclude that the accident had, at most, a small effect on US BWR operation, a conclusion reinforced by the absence of any discernible effect on BWR performance worldwide.

Babcock and Wilcox reactors

The final stage in the analysis of post-TMI reactor performance is an appraisal of the operation of those US PWRs for which Babcock and Wilcox (B & W) were the suppliers of the nuclear steam system, as was the case for both TMI-1 and TMI-2. There are nine B & W PWRs in the US

Table 4.3 *Load factor analysis for Babcock and Wilcox PWRs (excluding TMI-2)*

	Percentage mean annual load factor (Total mid-year capacity–GW)			Paired *t* statistics on quarterly load factors		
	78/79	79/80	80/81	78/79– 79/80	79/80– 80/81	78/79– 80/81
Including TMI-1	65.0	42.9	44.4	5.76	−0.44	2.93
	(6.3)	(7.3)	(7.3)			
Excluding TMI-1	63.8	49.8	51.6	2.32	−0.44	1.25
	(5.5)	(6.4)	(6.4)			

which were operational during the three-month period before 28 March 1979, including the two TMI reactors, and with such a small database particular care has to be exercised when interpreting results. In particular, the inclusion or otherwise of TMI-1 in the analysis significantly influences the results (TMI-2 is again omitted). We include the TMI-1 reactor in the analysis of B & W plant; it had operated satisfactorily for over four years before the accident and there is no technical reason why it should not generate electricity again in the future. Indeed, by the end of 1982, concerted efforts were being made by GPU, the utility responsible for the TMI reactors, to return unit 1 to service. Obviously, the effect of the prolonged TMI-1 outage is likely to be a major contributor to any reduction in performance of B & W PWRs. The results of the analysis are presented in the same way as before, with figure 4.3 showing three-monthly load factors and table 4.3 giving average annual load factors and paired *t* statistics.

The results presented in table 4.3 show that B & W reactors have been severely affected by the TMI accident. A drop of more than 22 percentage points in average load factor is observed in the twelve-month period following the accident compared with operation before the accident, and the difference in three-monthly load factors is correspondingly highly significant. In addition, any evidence of a recovery in performance in the second year after the accident is statistically very weak, pointing to possible longer-term problems with this reactor system. If the TMI-1 reactor is excluded from the analysis as a special case, the reduction in load factor amounts to 14 percentage points and is therefore in line with the analysis performed for worldwide PWR

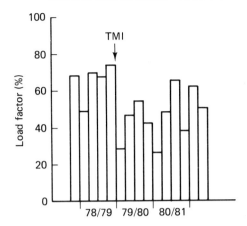

Figure 4.3 Quarterly load factors for Babcock and Wilcox PWRs (excluding TMI-2)

performance. However, the lack of recovery in performance in the second year after the accident persists even with the omission of TMI-1.

Individual responses

To summarise, we have shown that PWR load factors worldwide were significantly lower in the twelve-month period after March 1979 than they were before the TMI accident. The performance of reactors other than PWRs does not appear to have been affected but there is evidence to suggest that US nuclear stations have suffered to a somewhat greater extent than average. Although Babcock and Wilcox stations have performed particularly badly in the post-accident period, some of the effect is explained by the continued non-operation of the TMI-1 reactor. There is strong evidence of a recovery in PWR performance in the second year after the accident although annual load factors in March 1981 had not reached levels equivalent to those observed before the accident.

We must inject a note of caution. Our analysis has identified a drop in PWR performance post-TMI but has not proved any causal link. Indeed, there are some reactors whose fall in performance was not related to the accident (for example, the Surry reactors in the US, which suffered from steam generator problems during 1979). However, given the large database, comprising over 50 GW of PWR installed capacity worldwide, and accepting that certain plants were shut down because of specific technical problems both before and after the accident, it appears highly likely that a connection between the fall in performance and the TMI accident exists.

Further evidence to support this hypothesis comes from an International

Atomic Energy Agency (IAEA) publication[10] which lists the cause of all outages in 1979 for reactors operating in the member states. This shows that, for US B&W reactors, the poor performance post-TMI is directly attributable to the accident, and was the result of shutdowns imposed by the Nuclear Regulatory Commission (NRC) in which specified modifications and plant inspections were required. Evidence from Japan also points to a strong TMI-induced response. At the time of the accident only one Japanese reactor, the Ohi-1 PWR, was actually operating, but this was shut down for two months, again in direct response to the TMI accident.

Apart from these well-defined examples of cause and effect, the overall situation is less clear. However, a large number of PWRs experienced 'planned' refuelling and maintenance outages which extended beyond three months (compared with more normal annual outages of four to six weeks), and there was a high incidence of shutdowns imposed by regulatory authorities. Both of these facts lend weight to the idea that the performance of PWRs fell in the period immediately after March 1979 as a direct result of the TMI accident.

Cost implications of the fall in load factors

Having identified a significant deterioration in PWR performance in the Western world following TMI, it is possible to make some estimate of the resulting additional costs which have had to be met by utilities. We assume that the shortfall in PWR generation following TMI was met by coal-fired plant burning fuel of a fixed price. The price paid for coal by US utilities in 1978 was in the range 0.42 to 1.33 $ per GJ with an average value of 0.85 $ per GJ.[11] We use this coal price (equivalent to 1.2 $ per GJ in 1980 prices) for the two years following the TMI accident. With a value of 33% for the thermal efficiency of coal plant this coal price leads to a cost of 13 mills per kWh (1980 prices) for the fuel cost element of replacement coal-fired generation.

In 1978, the complete cost of LWR fuel in the US (i.e. including all stages of the fuel cycle from U_3O_8 feed to waste disposal) was in the region of 4.2 mills per kWh.[12] As a world average figure (which is closely tied to that in the US), we adopt a value of 6 mills per kWh (1980 prices) for the two years following TMI. It therefore follows, in this simplified approach, that each kWh of PWR generation lost due to utility action worldwide following the accident resulted in an additional cost of 7 mills.

We now turn to the magnitude of the reduction of PWR performance worldwide. From table 4.1, it may be seen that the average PWR load factor for the year 1979/80 is 13.7 percentage points lower than in the year before the accident and that the load factor for 1980/81 is 6.8 percentage points lower than the corresponding figure for 1978/79. If we conservatively assume that PWR performance worldwide had returned to pre-TMI levels by April 1981, then the total amount of generation lost may be obtained by combining these figures for drop in performance with the mid-year capacity figures given in table 4.1. The total obtained in this way amounts to 100 TWh which, at an additional cost of 7 mills per kWh, represents some $700 million (1980 prices).

There are a number of reasons for supposing that the figure of $700 million represents a lower limit. For example, we assumed that coal plant would be available to meet replacement generation, whereas some utilities would be forced to turn to high-cost oil-fired plant. We also chose a coal price near to the average US price and therefore took no account of the fact that US utilities which have opted for nuclear power generally serve areas where coal costs are higher than average. Also, the average cost of coal used in power stations was much lower in the US than in almost all other OECD countries (for example, the price of coal used in power stations in France in 1978 was over twice that of the US).[13] In addition, as we have already noted (p 79), the PWR load factor reduction was not limited to two years duration, as 1981/82 load factors were still below pre-TMI levels.

The major point which emerges from our analysis is that no nuclear utility can consider its operation to be independent of events in the nuclear industry worldwide. We have shown that an accident at one US reactor built by one of the smaller US NSSS suppliers has had a pronounced effect on PWR operation throughout the Western world. For this reason, we suggest that it is no longer the question of probabilities of large numbers of deaths following a catastrophic reactor accident that most concerns utility planners, since the safety record of the nuclear industry is undoubtedly good. Rather, the important issues for utilities now centre on the likelihood and total cost of much smaller accidents. Lessons have certainly been learnt as a result of TMI but the possibility of similar accidents occurring cannot reasonably be considered remote (as shown in the previous chapter); a similar but ultimately much less serious train of events occurred on 25 January 1982, at the Ginna PWR, also in the US.

These arguments have potentially important policy implications. In the next chapter we explore some of these implications by considering whether the possible worldwide impact of future reactor accidents is an issue which needs to be included in decisions concerning choice of reactor type.

5

Costs of nuclear accidents: implications for reactor choice

We have shown in the previous chapter that the TMI accident had economic consequences which were not restricted to the direct local costs (such as clean-up of the plant and replacement of lost generation from the TMI-2 reactor) but were felt worldwide. Because of the fall in perform- ance of PWRs in the wake of the accident, some of the costs of TMI have been borne by utilities which have not themselves suffered a nuclear accident, but have simply been operating PWRs. If this type of response is experienced after future accidents that are similar to, or more severe than, TMI, the expected costs of accidents could be a matter of some impor- tance in the choice of reactor system. This is especially so if these costs differ between reactor types.

However, the very low accident probabilities quoted for modern reactor systems could render this argument academic. In this chapter we attempt to discover whether this is so by quantifying the costs in the context of a decision on the type of nuclear reactor to be built in the UK. Since many of the numbers available are highly tentative, we limit our- selves to the modest objective of demonstrating whether the expected costs of accidents can safely be dismissed as being of no practical impor- tance in reactor choice.[1]

To estimate the importance of accident costs we define a quantity which we call the accident surcharge. This is the percentage increase in the capital cost of a nuclear station which exactly covers the expected economic consequences of reactor accidents throughout the lifetime of the station. This accident surcharge is analogous to a single-payment insurance premium. If collected by an external agency from the owners of each station, the agency would just have sufficient funds to compensate any utility unlucky enough to suffer from the adverse economic conse- quences of an accident. The absence of such an external agency in practice increases the importance of considering the accident surcharge on a par with the construction costs when deciding between reactor types.[2]

86

We distinguish between the direct and indirect elements of the surcharge. The direct element refers to the costs that will be incurred if the station in question should suffer an accident. The indirect element incorporates the costs incurred as a result of responses made by the operating utility to an accident elsewhere. For completeness we should calculate the accident surcharge as the integral of consequences times probabilities over all possible accidents.[3] This poses obvious computational difficulties, and we instead obtain an approximation to the accident surcharge by considering only a limited number of discrete classes of accident, which span the range between the worst experienced to date and the most severe reactor accident that could occur. The total accident surcharge that we calculate is then the sum of the direct and indirect elements, where each element is the sum of the probability times economic consequence for each class of accident. Given our limited objectives and the large uncertainties in the calculations, this discrete formulation of the problem does not introduce serious errors.

A UK example

As an illustration of how the calculation of a nuclear reactor accident surcharge may proceed, we consider an example based on the UK. We concentrate throughout on the PWR and the AGR, as these are the two principal contenders in the current debate concerning the choice of future reactor system in the UK. It would, however, be straightforward to extend the analysis to other reactor types, the Candu and BWR being particularly suitable candidates for inclusion.

We assume baseline values for several technical and economic parameters throughout, a complete list of which appears in table 5.1. For example, all the calculations are specific to a reactor, started in 1984, brought on line in 1994 (a likely date for the start of commercial operation of the first of the next generation of UK power reactors) and retired in 2024. Other important baseline assumptions include a 5% per annum growth rate of nuclear power in the Western world to 2025; the proportions of nuclear capacity remain at 58% PWRs, 2% AGRs as at present; all nuclear stations operate with a 60% load factor; and, perhaps most importantly, we assume that PWR and AGR reactors are equally safe.

We consider three discrete classes of accident, in increasing order of severity, and calculate the direct and indirect components of the accident surcharge for each class. Two elements are included in the direct cost component: clean-up costs and costs associated with replacing the damaged reactor in the electricity supply system. For the indirect costs, only one element is included explicitly, namely the cost of replacement

Table 5.1 *Baseline assumptions*

We list here the baseline assumptions that we use throughout the accident surcharge calculations.

Qualitative
Each reactor type is equally safe.
The accident surcharge is applied at the date at which the reactor comes on line.

Technical
Reactor construction commences 1984. Construction time 10 years, operating lifetime 30 years.
Lifetime load factor of 60%.
5% annual growth rate of Western world nuclear power capacity.
58% of installed nuclear capacity is provided by PWRs, 2% by AGRs, 40% others.
Future AGR reactors are 600 MW, all other reactors are 1200 MW.

Economic
1982 money values.
Exchange rate of £1 = $2.
5% annual discount rate.
Nuclear reactor capital cost 2×10^9 per GW for both PWRs and AGRs.
Nuclear fuel costs of 0.84 p/kWh generated; coal costs of 2.64 p/kWh generated.

generation which is necessary to offset shortfalls caused by reactors being shut down or de-rated in response to an accident somewhere in the world. No account is taken of other costs associated with the shut down of stations due, for example, to retrofitting which may be necessary to meet new regulatory requirements. Throughout our calculations, we make no attempt to quantify the extent of any possible adverse health effects attributable to accidents and consequently we exclude all costs which might be associated with such effects.

Class 1 accidents

We define a class 1 accident as one which is of similar severity to TMI. The quantities of radiation released off-site during such an accident would be small and would have little or no impact on the health of the local population.[4] The reactor itself would, however, suffer fairly extensive damage and would probably not operate again following the accident.

In estimating the frequency of class 1 accidents we turn to nuclear operating experience to date which includes the TMI accident. By the end of 1981, the total operating experience of commercial nuclear stations in the Western world was of the order of 1000 reactor years.[5] One plausible estimate of the frequency of class 1 reactor accidents would be one every

1000 reactor years of operation[6] but there are reasons for supposing that this estimate might be too high. In particular, it is likely that operators will learn by experience and that reactor safety will improve with time.[7] For this reason we assume a frequency of one per 5000 reactor years for future occurrences of class 1 type accidents for both PWRs and AGRs. Under our baseline assumptions of size of reactors and future nuclear power growth, this accident frequency implies that three class 1 accidents will occur during the 30-year operational life of a reactor due to come on-line in 1994.

Direct costs

The direct costs of the TMI accident are conservatively put at $2 billion (1982 prices), a figure which comprises around $1 billion for the clean-up operation at the plant (as outlined in Chapter 4) and a further $1 billion to account for the loss of a new reactor.[8] The gross electrical output of TMI-2 was 961 MW. In the light of experience following this accident we assume that the direct costs of a class 1 accident will be $1.5 billion for a 1 GW plant.[9] These costs are assumed to be proportional to the size of the plant.

The direct element of the accident surcharge is given by the accident probability multiplied by the direct cost of an accident. These extra costs, discounted to 1994 at 5% per annum, amount to 0.2% of capital costs at our baseline frequency of one class 1 accident in every 5000 reactor years. This figure applies to both PWRs and AGRs.

Indirect costs

Following the accident at TMI, load factors of PWRs worldwide fell, on average, by 13.7 percentage points in the first year after the accident and were still 6.8 percentage points below pre-accident performance levels in the second year after the accident, as we showed in the previous chapter. This lost generation had to be met by other types of generating plant, typically coal- or oil-fired, with higher fuel costs.

We assume that any future class 1 accident will produce an identical response to that witnessed post-TMI in reactors of the same type. We also assume, as observed following TMI, that reactors of a different type to the one which suffered the accident will not show a drop in performance.

To estimate the magnitude of the additional costs incurred it is necessary to know what type of plant will be used to meet the shortfall in generation. For a nuclear station coming on-line in the UK in the mid-1990s we assume that coal-fired stations will be used to compensate for reductions in nuclear generation following any future reactor accidents which may occur during the lifetime of the reactor.

Other key inputs necessary to calculate indirect accident costs are the cost of nuclear fuel and coal. We take single values which correspond to central UK Government estimates for fuel costs to electric utilities in the year 2000.[10] By adjusting the figures for inflation we obtain fuel costs in 1982 prices of 0.84 pence per kWh for nuclear and 2.64 pence per kWh for coal, a difference of 1.8 pence, or approximately 35 mills, per kWh. This difference is the quantity of interest, since nuclear fuel will be saved if the output of a reactor is reduced.

We multiply the replacement generation required (in kWh) by the additional costs incurred per kWh, to obtain a figure of $63 million for the indirect costs for each GW of nuclear plant in the UK of the same type as the one which suffered the accident. Under our baseline assumption that PWR and AGR reactors are equally safe, it is clear that accidents are more likely to occur at PWRs than AGRs simply because there are more of them in operation. For every class 1 accident that occurs in the Western world there is a 57% probability that the reactor is a PWR and a 4% probability that it is an AGR.[11] Therefore, the expected indirect costs of each class 1 accident per GW installed are $35.9 million for a UK PWR and $2.5 million for a UK AGR.

Our baseline accident frequency implies that three class 1 accidents will occur in the period 1994–2024. If the expected indirect accident costs are summed for each accident and discounted from the date of the accident to 1994, we obtain an indirect accident surcharge of 2.7% of capital costs for the PWR and 0.2% for the AGR. The difference in this indirect surcharge for class 1 accidents is due solely to the worldwide prominence of the PWR.

Class 2 accidents

We define our class 2 accident as one from which radiation doses equivalent to 1 emergency reference level (ERL) (e.g. 10 rem whole body dose) could be expected. We adopt this definition not because such a dose is of particular significance in itself, but because UK emergency regulations specify that evacuation of the local population is necessary if this dose level is reached.[12] Such an evacuation has never occurred in the history of nuclear power to date.[13]

We turn to nuclear design criteria to obtain an estimate for the frequency of such an accident. The latest nuclear stations in the UK are designed to a standard of 1 ERL in 10^4 reactor years of operation. We adopt this value for the frequency of class 2 accidents for both PWR and AGR designs, since this safety guideline would apply to either type of reactor if built in the UK. We recognise that the use of this value in the calculation of the indirect surcharge may underestimate the frequency of class 2 accidents in reactors of a previous generation, or in countries with less strict design criteria.

Direct costs

The experience in the USA following TMI provides a lower bound to the substantial costs that will be incurred at the site following a class 2 accident. We assume that the clean-up costs at a 1 GW station amount to $2 billion, twice our Chapter 4 estimate for TMI-2. Since it is doubtful whether TMI-2 will ever operate again, we assume that any reactor suffering a class 2 accident would be permanently shut down with no scrap or recovery value. This adds up to a further $2 billion per GW for the construction of replacement capacity.

Our assumed accident frequency translates to a 1 in 333 chance of a class 2 accident at each reactor during its lifetime. Allowing for the fact that such an accident could occur at any time from the date of commissioning until retirement 30 years later, we obtain direct surcharges for class 2 accidents of 0.2% of capital costs for both PWR and AGR.

Indirect costs

To calculate the indirect surcharge we concentrate on the effect of the first class 2 accident occurring somewhere in the world. With our baseline assumption of 5% annual growth in nuclear power use, there is a 17% chance of a class 2 accident during the ten-year construction time of a reactor started in 1984, and an 84% chance that such an accident will have occurred before the subsequent operating lifetime of the station is completed. The chances are that the first class 2 accident will occur in a PWR simply because of the worldwide PWR dominance. Under our baseline assumptions, there is a 57% probability that the first class 2 accident will occur in a PWR, a 4% probability for AGR and a 39% probability for some other type of reactor, as for class 1 accidents.

A wide range of responses to the first class 2 accident is possible. For our purpose it is the response of the CEGB and SSEB, the two UK utilities operating nuclear plant, that is relevant. The weakest response that we consider is similar to that experienced following TMI; a temporary drop in load factor for any reactor of the same type as the one involved in the accident, with no drop for other reactor types. This 'acceptance' response would again involve extra costs of $63 million per GW for replacement generation where a drop in load factor occurs. We also consider two stronger responses. The first involves the recognition that reactor systems have different characteristics. This 'discrimination' response would resemble 'acceptance' for all reactors except those of the same type as the station at which the accident occurred. Reactors of this type would be closed indefinitely. An even stronger reaction would be the 'rejection' response involving the permanent closure of all reactors following a class 2 accident at any station worldwide. Whilst these three responses by no means exhaust the possibilities, they enable a first calculation of this element of the surcharge to be made. We assume that the response of the UK utilities to the first class 2 accident stands a 2.5% chance of 'rejection', with a 5% chance of 'discrimination' and a 92.5% chance of the least severe 'acceptance' response. In using these probabilities we are making no judgement on the rationality of such responses, only on their likelihood.[14]

Evidence exists for the occurrence of discrimination between reactor types following TMI, the only class 1 accident to date; this leads us to make 'discrimination' the more likely of the two strong responses following a class 2 accident. We recognise the great uncertainty in these subjective probabilities; but we feel that the values we have chosen, with more than a 90% chance of a very limited response, are not unduly pessimistic.

The costs of a temporary drop in load factor are the same as if this occurs following a class 1 accident, about $63 million per GW. The costs incurred if a reactor is permanently closed are strongly dependent on when the premature closure occurs. If closure occurs towards the end of the reactor's planned life, replacement generation will only have to be provided for a few years, and the discounting of future expenditure will reduce this cost still further. To incorporate this, we have calculated the costs of permanent closure during construction, and after 5, 15 or 25 years of operation.[15] The indirect surcharge for class 2 accidents is then estimated by multiplying the probability of experiencing the first class 2 accident close to each of these four dates,[16] by the probability that the reactor will close or be de-rated,[17] and by the extra costs incurred. This gives an indirect surcharge for class 2 accidents of 3.9% for PWR and 1.7% for AGR.

Class 3 accidents

We define our class 3 accident as one leading to an uncontrolled release of radioactivity outside the plant. Current designs in the UK work to a standard of one class 3 accident in 10^6 reactor years of operation,[18] a value which we have adopted for the frequency of class 3 accidents for all types of reactor.

Direct costs

The direct element of the surcharge for class 3 accidents is negligible. Even if the costs were to be ten times those following a class 2 accident, the frequency is 100 times smaller, giving a direct surcharge less

Table 5.2 *Categories of reactor accident*

Accident category	Type	Frequency per reactor year	Response
Class 1	Similar severity to TMI	2×10^{-4}	100% A
Class 2	Radiation doses equivalent to 1 ERL (e.g. 10 rem whole body dose)	1×10^{-4}	$92\frac{1}{2}$% A 5% B $2\frac{1}{2}$% C
Class 3	Uncontrolled release of radioactivity	1×10^{-6}	25% A 50% B 25% C

Notes: Response A – load factor reduction of the same magnitude as that experienced post-TMI in all reactors similar to the one which suffered the accident; Response B – permanent closure of all reactors similar to the one which suffered the accident; and Response C – permanent closure of all reactors.

than 0.1% of capital costs. The most significant direct costs of a class 3 accident are likely to be the adverse health effects, which we make no attempt to evaluate.

Indirect costs

The indirect surcharge for class 3 accidents is calculated in much the same way as for class 2. The differences lie in the probability distribution of the time until the first accident, and in the likelihood of the various responses. Under our baseline assumptions, there is only a 1.8% chance of a class 3 accident occurring before the end of the 40-year construction and operating lifetime of stations currently being planned. However, if one does occur, we feel that it would require fairly exceptional circumstances to avoid a strong response by the UK utilities. We assume a 'rejection' probability of 25%, 'discrimination' 50% and 'acceptance' 25%. These values give indirect surcharges for class 3 accidents of 0.5% of capital costs for PWR, 0.3% for AGR.

The accident surcharge

We have suggested that a full appraisal of nuclear reactor economics should include a cost component, or accident surcharge, to account for the adverse financial consequences of future reactor accidents. The three categories of reactor accident considered are detailed in table 5.2. Calculations have been made for direct costs at the site, and for indirect costs due to actions taken in response to an accident elsewhere. The numerical

Table 5.3 *Accident surcharge for UK reactors (% of capital costs)*

Accident	Cost component	PWR	AGR
Class 1	Direct	0.2	0.2
	Indirect	2.7	0.2
Class 2	Direct	0.2	0.2
	Indirect	3.9	1.7
Class 3	Direct	—	—
	Indirect	0.5	0.3
Total accident surcharge		7.5	2.6

Note: — means less than 0.1

results, summarised in table 5.3, are specific to the UK where the next commercial nuclear power station to be ordered will be either a PWR or an AGR.

It is apparent from table 5.3 that the total accident surcharge cannot safely be dismissed as of no practical importance, being 7.5% of capital costs for PWRs and 2.6% for AGRs. The surcharge is dominated by indirect costs which differ from PWR to AGR, unlike the direct costs which are small and the same for both systems. The difference in the total accident surcharge amounts to almost 5% of capital costs; for comparison, the present capital cost advantage claimed for PWRs over AGRs is about 25%.

Sensitivity of our results

In calculating the accident surcharge figures presented in table 5.3 we have used a number of baseline assumptions. Significantly different conclusions may be reached by changing these assumptions, and some general discussion on the sensitivity of the results is necessary. Firstly we consider changes in our assumptions which will either reduce the magnitude of the surcharge or improve the relative position of the PWR.

(i) We have recognised that the frequency of accidents such as TMI will fall in the future as part of an anticipated learning process. As these class 1 accidents may become precursors to more serious accidents, it is possible that the frequency of class 2 and class 3 accidents will also fall with time. Any such drop in frequency would reduce the accident surcharge component due to these more serious types of accident. However, the frequencies used for class 2 and class 3 accidents have been taken from recent CEGB sources,[19] where it is recognised that these targets for the reliability of systems are very stringent and may not, in the event, be fully met.

(ii) We have assumed that subsequent accidents on the scale of TMI produce the same indirect response. It could be argued, however, that the post-TMI response was an irrational 'panic measure' which was perhaps to be expected following the first significant incident at a commercial reactor. Similar future accidents might result in much reduced knock-on effects which would reduce the accident surcharge.

(iii) Our responses to class 2 and class 3 accidents have necessarily been chosen subjectively and have taken account of the prolonged and widespread repercussions of TMI which extended far beyond a drop in load factor and appear to have had a significant effect on the nuclear industry worldwide. Nevertheless, the results are sensitive to our subjective accident responses and, if they have been overstated, the accident surcharge figures of table 5.3 will be overestimates.

(iv) In calculating the indirect accident costs we have assumed that other plant is available to meet shortfalls in generation. Under conditions of high electricity demand growth and low plant ordering in the UK, a situation could eventually occur in which no plant was available, particularly at peak periods of demand, to compensate for significant reductions in nuclear output. It may be less likely that operational reactors would be shut down or de-rated in the event of an accident if power black-outs were the results.[20]

(v) Throughout the chapter so far we have assumed that there is no difference in the safety of PWRs and AGRs. Given the large number of PWRs in operation worldwide and the wealth of operating experience with this system, which is expected to grow rapidly in the future, it may be argued that the PWR will be safer than the AGR. There is already evidence to suggest that an accident similar to the one at TMI was averted at the Ginna reactor in the US as operators benefited from knowledge and experience gained from the TMI accident.[21] If the PWR is a safer reactor its position relative to the AGR will be improved.

Just as some changes in assumptions lead to a reduction in the total accident surcharge or improve the relative position of the PWR, so other plausible changes increase the accident surcharge or improve the relative position of the AGR.

(i) Our baseline assumptions include a 5% per annum growth in nuclear capacity. If a higher growth rate for nuclear power is assumed the accident surcharge will be increased. This is because the number of accidents increases with the installed nuclear capacity, which results in a higher indirect component of the accident surcharge. A 5% per annum growth in nuclear capacity represents what many proponents of nuclear power would consider to be extremely slow progress. Even our low figures of Chapter 2 show a 5.6% per annum growth to the end of the century.

(ii) If, instead of coal-fired plant being available to meet generation shortfalls in the UK, one admits that some oil plant will be necessary to fill the gap, at least in the years to 2005, then indirect costs for all types of accident and for both types of reactor will be increased. This increase could be as much as 50% depending on coal/oil price differentials.

(iii) A contrary argument to the one presented above with regard to PWR safety may be made for AGRs. Although the operating experience obtained with AGRs is far less than with PWRs, there is some evidence to suggest that AGRs are intrinsically safer. This argument is not based on considerations of experience but lies in the basic physics and technology of the two systems.[22] In particular, it acknowledges that pre-stressed concrete pressure vessels are intrinsically safer than steel pressure vessels and that long response times under fault conditions, a feature of gas-graphite systems which have a high thermal inertia, imply a safer reactor.

(iv) We have taken no account of the problem of multiple units operating at a given reactor site. Following the accident at TMI both the unit 2 reactor, which suffered the accident, and the undamaged unit 1 reactor were shut down. Four years after the accident neither reactor had been returned to power. The continued shutdown of unit 1 represents a much stronger indirect response than we included in our calculation for class 1 accidents, and if this pattern is repeated, there will be an additional component to the accident surcharge for reactors at multiple unit sites.

(v) We have concentrated throughout on the economic costs of reactor accidents. We have made no attempt to put a value on the adverse health effects, which would increase the surcharge for both reactor types, possibly substantially.

As these discussions indicate, there exists a wide range of values for the accident surcharge, with the figures which we have presented being no more than the result of first calculations based on reasonable assumptions. However, it does seem clear that a surcharge which fully accounts for the adverse economic consequences of future reactor accidents will not necessarily be an insignificant element of total power station costs.

Policy implications

Our calculations of the reactor accident surcharge for the UK have shown that its magnitude may not be negligible and that it is smaller for AGRs than PWRs. Before discussing some of the implications of these results, we would first like to emphasise some points which are *not* implied by the analysis presented in this chapter:

(i) We do not conclude that PWRs are less safe than AGRs. All our numerical results are based on an assumption of equal safety.

(ii) We do not conclude that, because of their higher accident surcharge, PWRs should not be built in the UK. It is necessary to consider a large number of factors when deciding between two reactor systems. One of these factors, which we believe has been overlooked thus far, is the reactor accident surcharge.

(iii) We do not conclude that each new reactor to be built in the UK should be of a completely new design which will not suffer indirect effects from accidents at nuclear stations elsewhere in the world. The costs of such a strategy would far exceed any benefits that would result from reducing the reactor accident surcharge.

Nevertheless, we believe that this type of calculation of the accident surcharge is important and may have implications for future policy decisions. The surcharge cannot safely be dismissed as being negligible and should be included in economic evaluations of different reactor types. If such evaluations are to be made by power utilities, who are ultimately responsible for the generation of electricity at lowest cost (paying due regard to safety and environmental issues), the accident surcharge should be quantified with greater accuracy and completeness than we have attempted in the illustrative calculations presented in this chapter.

In recent years costs in the nuclear industry have been escalating rapidly, partly due to costs incurred in the pursuit of zero risk. This trend has become even more marked following TMI,[23] and helps to explain the dramatic downturn of nuclear ordering in many countries in the late 1970s and early 1980s, as highlighted in Chapter 2. For this reason it is necessary to know the value of the accident surcharge to decide how much effort and cost should be incurred in trying to improve safety at nuclear stations. Introducing extra safety measures to reduce the accident surcharge would be a sensible response, provided the measures satisfied the conventional economic test of marginal benefit exceeding marginal cost.

A further important point which emerges from our analysis is the fact that the largest element of the accident surcharge is the indirect effect of class 2 accidents.[24] This element reflects the possibility that utilities worldwide may be forced to close their reactors in response to an accident which is unlikely to cause any fatalities. The probability that reactors elsewhere may be forced to close as a result of an accident that kills no one is a reflection of the strong feelings engendered by nuclear power, for reasons unconnected with its actual safety record, and which we explore more fully in the next chapter.[25]

It may be that nuclear power will never be able to compete

economically with alternatives while these feelings persist. Such feelings increase the accident surcharge and lead to the incorporation of ever more costly safety devices to bring the surcharge back down to an acceptable level. As a result nuclear power is reaching the stage where, in some countries, it is becoming economically unattractive for electricity generation. We investigate this phenomenon in Chapter 7.

6

Defining the risks of nuclear power

The most commonly advocated method of comparing risks with other considerations is the economic theory of external costs. In this chapter we show that this theory runs into some serious difficulties if it is applied to nuclear power, and we propose an alternative method for defining risk. This broader definition is able to explain the continued concern about the risks of nuclear power. It also admits a greater range of valid risk-reduction activities, and we conclude the chapter by discussing which of these activities are likely to be most effective in reducing the risks of nuclear power.

The economic theory of external costs

An economist looking at the risks to human health imposed by an energy-producing technology would note two salient points:

(i)   The actors causing the increased risks (the risk imposers) do not, in general, have to pay compensation for the risks they cause.

(ii)   The actors on whom the increased risks fall (the risk receivers) do not, in general, have a choice about whether to accept the risks or not.

The normal conclusion of free market economics is that interpersonal trade in a commodity will only occur if it brings benefits to both sides and therefore society as a whole. Unfortunately, the lack of compensation and choice mean that this reassuring conclusion does not hold for risk. Without outside intervention, the imposition of risks can increase far beyond the stage where net benefits to society are obtained. If there is an absolute lack of compensation and choice, risks will continue to increase until the risk imposers would get no extra benefit from a higher level of risk. Since the risk receivers will be incurring substantial extra disbenefits (death being the ultimate disbenefit) from some of those risks, so too will society

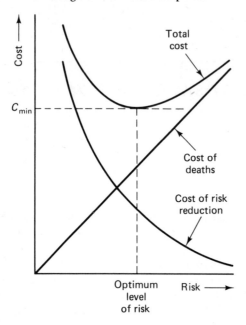

Figure 6.1 The economic theory of external costs applied to risk

as a whole. This unsatisfactory state of affairs clearly calls for inter-vention by some outside agency.[1] This role is usually adopted by some branch of government, and the economic theory of external costs is avail-able to help it reach an optimal outcome.

According to this economic theory, all levels of risk impose costs upon society due to the deaths caused among the risk receivers. In addition, costs are incurred by risk imposers in response to whatever standards of safety are introduced by the government agency.[2] These risk-reducing responses normally involve changing methods of production or reducing output. The extra costs incurred are real costs to society, not just transfers from one group to another. The two sets of costs are shown in figure 6.1. The level of risk that the government permits an industry to impose is shown along the horizontal axis. The lower this level, the lower the costs due to deaths amongst the risk receivers, and the higher the costs due to risk reduction responses amongst the risk imposers, and vice versa. The total cost to society is the sum of these two sets of costs. This is also shown in figure 6.1. At some level of risk, this total cost will go through a minimum. This level of risk is optimal for society as a whole. The govern-ment agency should design its safety standards or tax structure with the aim of ending up at this optimum level of risk.[3]

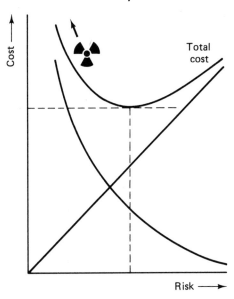

Figure 6.2 The risk of death from nuclear power

This method of balancing conflicting objectives to achieve an overall optimum has great merit in many fields. What happens if we try to fit nuclear power risks into this scheme? On any sensible valuation, the safety standards presently achieved by operators of nuclear plant, locate nuclear power on the rising part of the total cost curve as shown in figure 6.2. For example, the valuation of each life saved would need to be somewhere between $18 million and $1000 million to justify present plans for burying high level waste in stable geological formations rather than continuing to dispose of it in deep ocean areas. In non-energy activities, implicit or explicit valuations of a few thousand dollars to $2 million per life saved are typically employed.[4] Despite this, the inexorable pressure from public and government is pushing nuclear power towards ever more stringent safety standards as shown by the arrow in figure 6.2.[5] This pressure will continue to lead nuclear power further away from the optimum suggested by the economic theory of external costs, in exact contradiction to the predictions of the theory. The typical response of the economist to this is either to admit the anomalous result presented by nuclear power, or to cite the stupidity of the public as evidence of the need for further education campaigns.[6] It is clear to us that the anomalous position of nuclear power shows that the theory is incomplete.

Defining risk

Economics fails to predict the optimal level of risk from nuclear power, because its practitioners assume that the meaning of risk can be unambiguously and objectively defined. This is the source of many difficulties.[7] By providing a better definition of risk we can aim to account for nuclear power while retaining the narrower theory as a special case.

Many studies of the hazards from energy production use the terms 'risk' and 'deaths per GWyr' interchangeably as though it was obvious that this is what risk means.[8] But is it obvious?

(i) An 80-year-old woman dies peacefully in bed. An 18-year-old girl dies in a motorcycle accident. Are both deaths equally tragic, or should some account be taken of the comparatively small loss of life expectancy in the first case?[9]

(ii) A worker on a North Sea oil rig, earning three times the average wage for his profession, is killed. A member of the public is killed in a collision with a truck distributing oil products. Should both deaths count equally against oil production, or has the worker not already received some compensation through higher wages? Would it not be double counting against the oil industry to refuse to take this into account?

(iii) One miner dies instantly from a roof fall in a pit. A thousand more are incapacitated for life by diseases resulting from the inhalation of coal dust. Should the death count against the coal industry while the illnesses pass by uncounted, or should our index of risks not take some notice of morbidity[10] as well as death?

These examples show that at the very least there is a case to be made for separating out three elements – public deaths, worker deaths and morbidity – when defining the risks from energy production. An ideal procedure would go much further and examine the age groups at risk, the suffering caused by each illness or accident, and the exact level of wages being received in compensation, but this would involve trying to run before we have learned to walk. The proposed separation of just three elements is sufficient to demonstrate that it is far from obvious what risk means. Rather than attempting a finer subdivision of these aspects, it is more important to introduce a totally different dimension if we are to capture the essence of the risks from energy production.

It is quite clear that the expected deaths and illnesses from a technology are necessary but not sufficient to describe its risk to human health. Two technologies that score identically on these measures can be viewed quite differently by people asked to evaluate the severity of their risks. This phenomenon is so striking that some effort has been devoted to attempts at explanation. If two technologies cause identical expected deaths and morbidity, it has been suggested that the technology which will cause the greater anxiety will be the one which

(i)   is imposed involuntarily rather than adopted voluntarily[11]
(ii)   causes the expected number of deaths in a few catastrophic accidents rather than at a steady predictable rate
(iii)   is new – old and familiar technologies have given people time to adjust to their risks
(iv)   is certain to be fatal should something go wrong – people prefer to have a sporting chance of escaping death by their own actions
(v)   is not controllable by those exposed to risk
(vi)   has risks that are subject to a large margin of uncertainty, rather than being known precisely by those in charge of the technology.

This is an impressive array of factors other than expected deaths and morbidity that are considered to enter into the risks from a technology, and the above list is by no means complete. Since we are seeking a simple way of representing risks, it would be inconvenient if we had to work out how badly each technology performs against each of these criteria.

Fortunately, this is unlikely to be necessary. The factors which have been proposed to account for the anxiety engendered by a technology seem to be highly intercorrelated. In our list of six, for example, a technology that is new is almost certain to have risks that are subject to great uncertainty and vice versa, so factors (iii) and (vi) are really just different expressions of some superfactor A. Likewise, technologies that are imposed involuntarily are unlikely to be controllable by those on the receiving end of the risk. Research in the USA has shown that all the factors proposed to account for increased anxiety can be replaced by two superfactors with very little loss of explanatory power.[12] While these superfactors are strictly speaking just mathematical constructs that arise from factor analysis, they can be given descriptive names to convey some sense of the concern captured in each. The first is therefore labelled the 'unknown' nature of the technology. This superfactor is highly correlated with novelty, uncertainty, involuntariness, and uncontrollability, which all tend to go together. The second expresses the degree to which a technology evokes a feeling of 'dread' and is correlated with catastrophic accidents and certainty of death. The former might be seen as expressing aversion to uncertainty, thus representing the intellectual aspects of concern. The latter captures more of the ability of a technology to evoke a visceral response. Together they can account for over 80% of the variation in anxiety caused by technologies with identical numbers of expected deaths and morbidity. We assume these two superfactors to be sufficient complementary measures of concern.

Thus we consider that the risk of any energy-producing technology depends on how badly it scores on the five attributes of risk that we have identified:

(i)   Expected number of deaths amongst members of the public per unit of output.

(ii)   Expected number of deaths amongst workers in the industry per unit of output.

(iii) Expected level of morbidity per unit of output.

(iv)   The extent to which the technology is unknown, representing intellectual aversion to uncertainty.

(v)   The extent to which the technology is dread, representing gut-reaction dislike.

The higher the score of a technology on each one of these attributes, the higher its risk, all other things equal.

We could just stop at this point. Our prescription for describing the risk from any technology would then read: 'Obtain the score of the technology on each of these five attributes and write it as a vector with five elements. You now have all the information you need to decide how risky the technology is.' The risk vector for energy producing technology I might then be (1, 0.5, 6000, 80, 90). The individual entries indicate that technology I is expected to cause 1 death amongst members of the public, 0.5 of a death amongst workers in the industry and 6000 person-days of incapacity per GWyr of output. It scores 80 out of a possible 100 on the 'unknown' attribute, and 90 out of a possible 100 on dread.[13]

But this prescription is not really helpful. The driving force behind obtaining a more complete expression of risk is the desire to make decisions between technologies. Inevitably we are going to have to decide between technology I and technology II, which might have a risk vector of (8, 3, 12000, 70, 50). Technology II scores better than I on some attributes of risk (unknown and dread) and worse on the others. We need to balance one attribute against another somehow if we are to reach any decision.[14] Leaving risk defined only as a vector with five elements forces this balancing to be performed intuitively by saying, for instance, 'Well I just like the look of this risk vector more than that one.' This is the worst of all worlds. Vectors are quite complicated to manipulate mentally. Intuitive weighting opens the door to errors both arithmetical[15] and logical.[16] Worse still, the values underlying the intuitive aggregation remain hidden, and so no debate can occur about whether the implicit weighting, for instance, of a worker death against a public death is reasonable.

Since we believe the underlying value structure to be one of the more important issues in the discussion of risks, we prefer to create a single numerical index of risk from the five elements of the risk vector. To be useful, the risk index must have the property that the riskier a technology, the higher its risk index. Then we can say that if the risk index of I is higher than that of competing technology II, I should only be pursued if its benefits exceed its costs by a correspondingly larger amount.

The simplest way of aggregating explicitly is to assign a multiplicative weight to each element of the risk vector and sum the resulting weighted scores.[17] The validity of this procedure depends on two behavioural assumptions that do not seem unreasonable, and may be satisfactory for our purpose. The first of these is that tradeoffs between two of the attributes of risk should not depend on the level of other attributes. For instance, a willingness to accept one extra public death to save the lives of two workers in the industry when the level of morbidity is 6000 person-days of incapacity per GWyr should not change if the level of morbidity rises to 12000. The second is that preferences amongst different gambles inside one attribute should not depend on the level of other attributes. The simplest way of ensuring this second condition is to assume a neutral attitude to uncertainty inside each attribute (e.g. the certainty of one public death is just as bad as a 1 in 100 chance of 100 public deaths except in so far as the second presumably scores worse on the dread attribute), and this is the route we adopt.

If it can be validly used, this weighted additive form has enormous flexibility. It can accommodate any set of risky attributes, any scheme for scoring those attributes, and any set of relative weights for the different attributes. As such, it is not so much an index as a scheme for generating a family of indices. In the following section, we generate several members of this family and examine how sensitive the relative riskiness of different energy technologies is to choice of the definition of risk.

Risk indices of energy technologies

Before producing a family of risk indices and applying them to a sample of energy technologies, we restate the role that the results of this analysis would play in the choice of technologies. In making such a decision, it would be necessary to combine risks with all other relevant consequences. As suggested by figure 6.3, the space of possible consequences can be thought of as falling into three major sub-categories: (a) net economic effects, the difference between the benefits and the non-risk costs of a project; (b) the environmental effects, those (positive and negative) impacts that are borne by the environment without an immediate effect on people's finances or health; and (c) risky consequences, with which we are at present concerned.

We now consider the risks of six energy technologies. Five of these, coal, hydropower, large-scale windpower, small-scale windpower, and

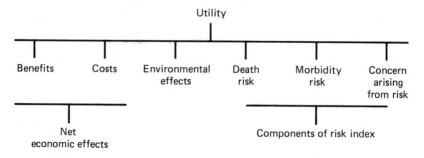

Figure 6.3 Attributes of consequence for choice of technology

Figure 6.4 Attributes of consequence for risk index

nuclear power, can be employed to increase the supply of electricity. The sixth, energy conservation, can reduce the demand for electricity, thereby freeing existing supplies for other uses. The technical aspects of electricity supply are documented elsewhere,[18] and we discuss the economic risks and benefits associated with nuclear power in other chapters. We concentrate here on the risks to human health.

The five attributes of risk that we incorporate into our index are shown in figure 6.4. The first is the number of deaths caused amongst members of the public by the construction and operation of the technology. The second is the number of deaths amongst workers involved in the industry. Separating public from occupational deaths allows a different weight to be placed upon each. We measure both these consequences by the number of deaths per GWyr of electricity generated or saved. The third element of our risk index is the morbidity caused by the construction and operation of the technology. We measure this element by the person-days of incapacity caused per GWyr of electricity. Our final two attributes capture the concern engendered by the construction and operation of the technology.

The scales that we use for scoring the five attributes are as follows. A score of zero on attributes one to three indicates a technology that produces no casualties (i.e. death, illness or injury to workers or public).

Table 6.1 *The components of attributes four and five*

Attribute	Score of zero implies technology has these properties	Score of 100 implies technology has these properties
4 Unknown risk	Voluntary	Involuntary
	Observable	Not observable
	Known to exposed	Unknown to exposed
	Effect immediate	Effect delayed
	Old	New
	Known to science	Unknown to science
	Controllable	Uncontrollable
5 Dread risk	Consequences not fatal	Consequences fatal
	Equitable	Not equitable
	Individual	Catastrophic
	Low future risk	High future risk
	Easily reduced	Not easily reduced
	Decreasing	Increasing
	Doesn't affect me	Affects me

Although a natural anchor for a casualty scale, zero is unachievable in practice. At the other end of the scale, scores of 100 on attributes one and two are defined, respectively, as an expectation of 10 public and 10 occupational deaths per GWyr of electricity generated or saved. Sixty thousand person-days of incapacity per GWyr would merit a score of 100 on attribute three. These values are meant to be roughly equal to the worst risks actually encountered with conceivable energy systems.

The characteristics that would give scores of zero and 100 on attributes four (unknown risk) and five (dread risk) are shown in table 6.1. Research has shown that although no technology quite reaches either extreme, mountain climbing and handguns score close to zero on attribute four (at least for subjects in the USA), as do home appliances and football on attribute five. At the other extreme, DNA research is rated as sufficiently unknown to receive a score in the nineties on attribute four, while nuclear weapons do likewise on attribute five.[19]

The next step in constructing a risk index is to score each technology on each attribute. In this scoring, the anticipated effects are translated into a numerical scale so that any given increment on the scale is of equal significance (e.g. going from 10 to 20 is as bad as going from 75 to 85). This is a judgemental procedure, based upon the available research results. Hence, some disagreement is to be expected. In the absence of consensus, we could use either the best guess of a single individual, or

Table 6.2 *The scores of the six technologies*

Attribute	Coal	Hydro	Large-scale wind	Small-scale wind	Nuclear	Conser-vation
1. Public deaths	80	10	20	5	10	5
2. Occupational deaths	30	20	10	30	5	10
3. Morbidity	20	20	40	50	10	40
4. Unknown risk	70	60	90	50	80	40
5. Dread risk	50	50	40	20	90	10

varied values reflecting the diversity of expert opinion. In the latter case, we could conduct a sensitivity analysis, recalculating the risk index with high and low estimates, in order to see how sensitive the ranking of technologies is to these differences in opinion. Alternatively, we could try to determine the distribution of expert opinion and incorporate the whole distribution in order to simulate 'what the experts think'.

In fact we simply use point estimates derived from a reading of relevant publications.[20] We found considerable differences of opinion in this literature. For example, the extreme values for occupational deaths for coal were 0.7 and 8 deaths per GWyr of electricity generated. The scores in table 6.2 are within the range found for each attribute. We found very little data on two technologies: small-scale windpower and conservation; the scores for these are subjectively adapted from other technologies. For example, the score for conservation on attributes four and five is an average of the scores given by respondents for home appliances and bicycles. These numbers should not be considered to be definitive, but we believe that readers will find them credible.

The final step in specifying the risk index is to assign weights to the different risk attributes. As these weights reflect value judgements, dis-agreements are legitimate and to be expected. We have, therefore, developed four separate sets of weights designed to illustrate four of the perspectives that people might adopt. These are labelled A to D in table 6.3. For each, the set of weights sums to 1, and may be interpreted as an allocation of importance over the different attributes.

Brief descriptions will explain the view that could motivate the adop-tion of each set. Set A rejects anything but readily measured physiological effects; treats a death as a death, whether it befalls a worker or a member of the public; views a life as equal to 6000 person-days of incapacity. This is the set of weights that has been implicitly used in much of the recent comparative risk literature that does not simply treat risk as equivalent to

Table 6.3 *Four possible sets of weights*

Attribute	A	B	C	D
1. Public deaths	0.33	0.40	0.20	0.08
2. Occupational deaths	0.33	0.20	0.05	0.04
3. Morbidity	0.33	0.20	0.05	0.40
4. Unknown risk	0	0.10	0.30	0.24
5. Dread risk	0	0.10	0.40	0.24
Sum of weights	1	1	1	1

expected death.[21] Many workers, including some nuclear proponents, are now coming to realise this set of weights is too narrow.[22] Set B reflects a belief that anxiety should be taken into account; that public deaths should be twice as important as worker deaths (perhaps because of the elements of choice and compensation in the workers' risk) and that a worker death should still be treated as equivalent to the loss of 6000 person-days. Set C increases the ratio of weights for public to occupational deaths and assigns major importance to concern. The specific weights imply a willingness to trade off 10 public deaths per GWyr to move from a technology causing extreme dread to one that is about average, perhaps feeling that the toll from concern-generated stress is large, or that even minor accidents in dreaded technologies can cause social and economic disruption that is enormously costly. The D weights represent a paramount concern with the suffering of the living through injury or anxiety, rather than with the number of deaths.

Given these values and weights, it is computationally simple to calculate the risk from these different technologies. For example, the risk from coal using Set A weights is $0.33(80) + 0.33(30) + 0.33(20) = 42.9$. Because we have standardised the scores to range from 0 to 100 and the weights to sum to 1, it is possible to compare risk indices across technologies and across weighting schemes.

The resulting index numbers are shown in figure 6.5. Those for coal, small-scale windpower and conservation vary little across the sets of weights that we have investigated, whilst those for hydropower, large-scale windpower and particularly nuclear power vary much more. That is, if one accepts the consequence estimates expressed in the scores of table 6.2, then the riskiness of these last three technologies depends greatly upon the importance given to the different attributes. Table 6.4 shows another reflection of this sensitivity. Coal ranks consistently badly, whereas nuclear may be best or worst depending upon the set of weights

Table 6.4 *Ranking the risk from the six technologies*

		Set of weights			
	Rank	A	B	C	D
Best	1	*Nuclear*	Conservation	Conservation	Conservation
	2	Hydro	Hydro	Small wind	Hydro
	3	Conservation	*Nuclear*	Hydro	Small wind
	4	Large wind	Small wind	Large wind	Coal
	5	Small wind	Large wind	Coal	*Nuclear*
Worst	6	Coal	Coal	*Nuclear*	Large wind

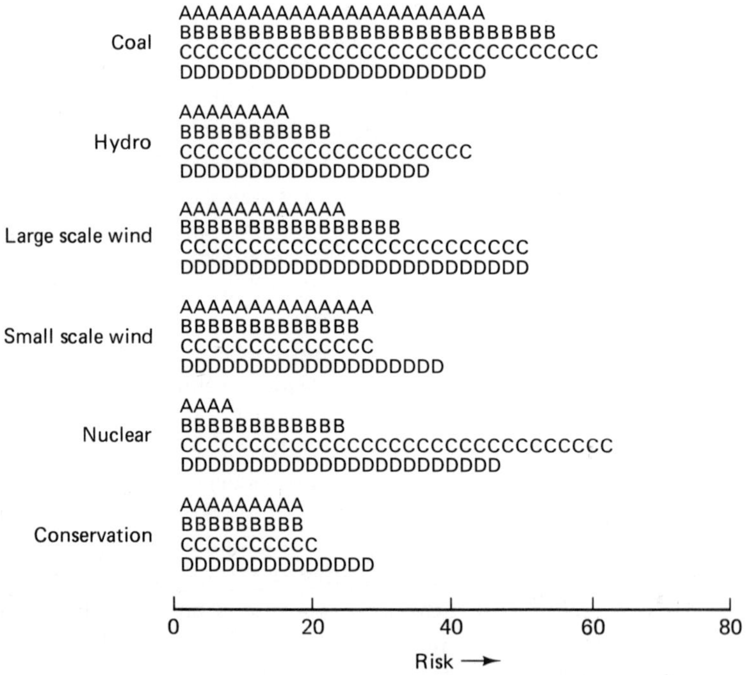

Coal
```
AAAAAAAAAAAAAAAAAAAAAAA
BBBBBBBBBBBBBBBBBBBBBBBBBB
CCCCCCCCCCCCCCCCCCCCCCCCCCCCC
DDDDDDDDDDDDDDDDDDDDDD
```

Hydro
```
AAAAAAAA
BBBBBBBBBBB
CCCCCCCCCCCCCCCCCCCCC
DDDDDDDDDDDDDDDDDD
```

Large scale wind
```
AAAAAAAAAAA
BBBBBBBBBBBBBBBB
CCCCCCCCCCCCCCCCCCCCCCCCC
DDDDDDDDDDDDDDDDDDDDDDDDDD
```

Small scale wind
```
AAAAAAAAAAAAA
BBBBBBBBBBBBB
CCCCCCCCCCCCCC
DDDDDDDDDDDDDDDDDD
```

Nuclear
```
AAAA
BBBBBBBBBBB
CCCCCCCCCCCCCCCCCCCCCCCCCCCCCCCCC
DDDDDDDDDDDDDDDDDDDDDDDD
```

Conservation
```
AAAAAAAAA
BBBBBBBBB
CCCCCCCCC
DDDDDDDDDDDDDD
```

```
0        20        40        60        80
                  Risk ➝
```

Figure 6.5 The risk indices of the six technologies on four sets of weights A, B, C, D

used. These variations occur despite complete agreement regarding the magnitude of the different consequences, as expressed in the single set of scores that we have used. Thus, arguments over riskiness may reflect only disagreements about values.

Some readers may be unhappy with our illustrative sets of weights; they can substitute their own and easily repeat the analysis. We are concerned not to produce another institutionalised magic number that is carved in tablets of stone and produced whenever debates about nuclear power degenerate into propaganda. That is one of the reasons we have calculated risk indices with several sets of weights.[23] There is no guarantee that a consensus over weights will increase as time progresses. A public debate over what position society should adopt is a prerequisite for such a consensus to emerge.

Risk reduction

Many scientists may be unwilling to adopt our broadened definition of risk because of this apparent removal of risk from the arena of their special competence. In particular, nuclear proponents may view any scheme that accepts as valid a high risk index for nuclear power, as a very dark cloud on the horizon. However, once the broader definition of risk is accepted, a silver lining to the cloud does emerge, in the shape of the range of valid risk-reduction activities that are opened up. Under our scheme, proponents of any technology who discover the climate of opinion turning against their choice, because of its risks, now have at least four options open.

(i) To attempt to reduce the scores of their technology on the death and morbidity attributes of risk. This is the route that has traditionally been taken. Indeed it is the only risk-reduction activity recognised as valid by narrower definitions that equate risk to deaths per unit of output, and use the economic theory of external costs to combine risks with other attributes of the technology.

(ii) To try to reduce the anxiety engendered by their technology. The factors that cause anxiety to increase are becoming more clear. We listed a number of them in table 6.1. As a consequence, the most promising areas for any attempts to reduce the anxiety caused by a technology are coming into sharper focus.

(iii) Proponents can argue that undue weight has been placed upon attributes of risk where their technology scores badly. Since the weights emerge from underlying value systems, this debate can be expected to range far from its starting place of energy policy.

(iv) We have already stressed that, before a decision between energy supply technologies can be taken, risks must be combined with net economic costs, environmental effects and any other consequences. If the popular consensus is tending to emphasise the risks, proponents of a technology can widen the debate by claiming that undue weight is being placed upon risk as opposed to other consequences. Once again this debate is likely to range over territory not normally seen as central to energy policy formation.

Since the late 1970s the popular consensus seems to have been moving in the direction of the C set of weights, which show the risks from nuclear power in a very poor light. We can use our broadened definition of risk to suggest which of these risk reduction options holds the greatest promise for nuclear proponents if this movement should continue. The risk index of nuclear power on the C set of weights is 62.75; the contribution of expected deaths and morbidity towards this total is a mere 2.75. It is therefore clear that to try to reduce the already low scores on the expected deaths and morbidity attributes is the least promising option for nuclear proponents. The nuclear scores on these attributes are so low at present because a great deal of effort has already been expended; further improvements would be difficult and expensive to achieve. Yet this is exactly where effort has been and continues to be concentrated. In the UK this has led to the inclusion of a secondary containment building in the Sizewell PWR design plans, at an additional cost estimated to be in the region of £10 million.[24] In the USA, plans are being advanced for super-safe reactors in an attempt to win back public confidence.[25] What this will do to the estimated cost of nuclear power has not been specified.

In view of the notable lack of success of these efforts to reduce the total risk from nuclear power, there would seem to be a good case for increasing the emphasis on some or all of the other three options for risk reduction. Attempting to reduce the scores of nuclear power on the anxiety attributes could be the best option. This may sound like the familiar plea for better public education in matters of nuclear safety, merely obfuscated by complex arguments. But there is one crucial difference. Those who take a narrow view of risk feel that the primary problem is public education. They believe that even if they are unable to educate the public, nuclear power will be able to be forced through because of its low 'objective' risk. They will therefore continue to put a low priority on public education right up to the day that nuclear power is rejected by public consensus, expressed directly or through the ballot box. Our broader definition of risk accepts the validity of opinions that nuclear power has a high total risk. Nuclear proponents are quite free to argue their case for lower scores or lower weights on the anxiety attributes. If they are unable to persuade the public of the justice of their case, our definition recognises the political reality that it is the experts rather than the public who must give way. As free market economists realised long ago, nothing concentrates the mind better than the knowledge that failure will mean the end of the enterprise. Adopting a broader definition of risk might prove to be just the spur required to prevent this fate befalling nuclear power.

7

The uncertain economics of a nuclear power programme

In Chapter 1 we pointed out that increasingly demanding safety standards have had a major impact on the capital costs of nuclear stations. We also compared the overall economics of nuclear power, as seen in the early 1980s, with perceptions held in the halcyon days of the early 1970s, when nuclear power was widely heralded as a universal solution to world energy problems. The contrast was highlighted in Chapter 2, where specific examples illustrated the extent to which nuclear power has fallen from grace in a large number of countries.

In this chapter we take the debate concerning the future economic viability of nuclear power one stage further, not simply by questioning *whether* the economics will be attractive, but by explicitly addressing the question: 'What is the *likelihood* of nuclear-generated electricity proving economic?' In other words, we are admitting uncertainty into the argument and are asking the reader to accept that any long-term view of the future cannot rely on single-valued estimates for a large number of uncertain, and often little-understood, variables.

Consider, for example, nuclear plant capital costs. We have seen, in Chapter 1, the extent to which real costs rose during the 1970s in the USA; a rise that was mirrored in most Western countries. For a utility deciding whether to build a reactor now, for operation in the early 1990s, it is important to know the extent to which historic cost escalation is likely to continue in the future. Some authors have suggested[1] that extrapolation of past trends is justified, as little evidence exists to suggest that programmes involving costly backfitting and upgrading of safety systems are now on the decline. An alternative viewpoint would suggest that most of the cost increases have already taken place, safe and mature reactor designs now exist, and confidence may be placed in recently produced capital cost estimates.[2]

We can see elements of truth in both arguments, and therefore feel that to adopt either viewpoint dogmatically would be unsupportable. We prefer an evaluation of capital costs which recognises that any viewpoint is subject to uncertainty, and take account of this by using a probability distribution of costs. The shape and parametrisation of such a distribution is subjective – as agreement is seldom reached on the choice of a single value for an important variable, it is unreasonable to assume that agreement over the degree of uncertainty will be forthcoming. Nevertheless, by admitting uncertainty into calculations of nuclear power economics (not simply with regard to capital costs but also for a wide range of other variables such as the future price of competing fossil fuels), we take a step forward and, hopefully, extend the debate beyond the entrenched positions held by both proponents and opponents of nuclear power.

Sensitivity analysis

In its widest sense, sensitivity analysis is the examination of the variation of the result, or output, from some calculation, to changes made to input variables. The magnitude of the changes reflects the degree of uncertainty surrounding each of the variables. This type of problem has been dealt with at length in the natural sciences,[3] and even in the energy field it is not new. The incorporation of uncertainty into economic appraisals of energy projects is undertaken routinely, but in many cases sensitivity analyses have been restricted to changing variables on a one-at-a-time basis and varying them over limited ranges.[4]

The alternative approach of scenario analysis has much to commend it. With this technique a number of plausible background views or scenarios are proposed, and the outcome of the project under investigation is examined against the alternative backgrounds. One of the major drawbacks of the method is that the central scenario frequently assumes an overwhelming importance which tends to negate the original rationale for exploring more than one outcome.

The situations in which energy planning has appeared most inadequate, when examined with the benefit of hindsight, are those in which either uncertainty was not explored or, if it was considered, only small deviations from a central trend were admitted. The classic examples may be found in decisions made just before the first oil shock of 1973.[5] Of the few astute observers who anticipated a large rise in the world oil price, none entertained the view that a fourfold increase within a period of just three months[6] was around the corner.

Whether any current scenario or sensitivity analysis methodology could have led to the adoption of investment plans which remained robust in the wake of the first oil price rise, is questionable. Nevertheless, the underlying message that uncertainty is important and has frequently been underestimated in the energy field, now has widespread acceptance.[7]

Investment planning in the electricity sector

When energy modellers turn their attention to the problem of electricity supply, the general approach adopted is to find some least-cost capacity expansion programme which will satisfy projected demand for some years in the future. Within this broad framework, linear programming techniques have found widespread applicability, thanks originally to system planners working for EDF in France.[8]

A linear programming (LP) approach is one in which a linear function is optimised subject to a number of linear constraints. The theoretical formulation and solution of this class of problems dates from the years immediately following the Second World War,[9] when it was recognised that a number of military and strategic problems came within this overall framework.[10]

In the case of electricity investment planning, the problem is to determine what mix of generating plant will minimise total costs given various physical constraints that apply in any supply network.[11] In its simplest form the problem may be stated as follows:

For the whole system, over the entire planning period minimise

Capital costs + fuel costs + non-fuel operating costs

subject to the constraints:

- electricity demand is met;
- sufficient capacity exists on the system to ensure adequate supply security;
- the output of any plant is limited by its availability.

By supplying information on all the generating plant options under consideration (capital costs, fuel and non-fuel running costs, availabilities), along with future levels of electricity demand, a unique optimal planting programme will be selected. This programme need not result in a single type of plant being constructed, as the nature of electricity demand (high peak demand for short periods at particular times of day and certain seasons of the year, along with a much smaller, baseload demand, present even at times of lowest electricity consumption), and the different capital and running cost characteristics of the various plant options, lead to an optimal mix of different plant types. In addition, other constraints may limit the total capacity of a given type of generating plant (for example, there may be a limit to the number of sites suitable for hydro projects). However, as far as selecting plant for baseload operation is concerned, some preferred option will emerge from the possibilities under consideration, which could, for example, include nuclear power, coal-fired stations, or oil-fired plant.

To explore uncertainty within this modelling framework, it is necessary to replace single values for input variables with probability distributions. This can be done for every input variable required by the model, or, alternatively, a subset may be selected and other variables, which are known to have a minimal effect on the solution, can be represented by single values.

A UK example

An example illustrates how this procedure works in practice. We again consider the system of the Central Electricity Generating Board (CEGB), the utility responsible for the generation and supply of electricity in England and Wales. There are currently three principal options open to the CEGB concerning the choice of future baseload plant, namely, coal-fired stations, PWRs (the US Westinghouse design being favoured) or the British-built AGRs.[12] It is uncertain which of the three represents the least-cost option and, if it turns out to be the PWR, whether a major programme of PWR construction is justified, as advocated by some of its proponents. The key variables which most influence the choice of least-cost plant are capital costs, running costs and plant performance (expressed as an availability figure).

The CEGB has presented its views on each of the key variables and has explored the impact of small changes to their central estimates. They conclude that the least-cost option is the PWR and advocate building such a station at Sizewell in Suffolk.[13] What happens when we bring our broader view of uncertainty into the argument?

Turning first to capital costs we find that there are a number of reasons for supposing that official figures may not, in the event, turn out to be true central estimates and that uncertainty may have been underestimated. In recent years the final costs of completed stations have consistently exceeded the original estimates (after allowing for inflation). For coal-fired stations brought on-line between 1966 and 1974 the average ratio of final costs to the estimate made at the time of the investment commitment was 1.2, whereas for the four AGR stations built by the CEGB, latest estimates of this ratio lie in the range 1.3 to 2.6.[14] The CEGB has no experience of building PWRs.

In the light of these cost overruns, we feel that the CEGB's view of uncertainty, in which all current estimates are seen as central values and actual outcomes are thought unlikely to lie outside the range ±12% for coal plant or ±15% for AGRs and PWRs, is in serious danger of both

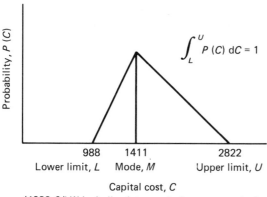

Figure 7.1 Probability distribution of PWR capital costs

underestimating uncertainty and erring on the side of optimism. The probability distributions that we choose for capital costs take these reservations into account.

As far as the shape of the distributions is concerned, a triangular representation is adopted. This enables asymmetries to be incorporated, and, for our subjective view on PWR capital costs, for example, leads to the choice of the probability distribution shown in figure 7.1. The mode of the distribution is simply the CEGB central estimate, the upper bound is twice this estimate and the lower bound 70% of the CEGB figure. We have therefore adopted a view on PWR capital costs in which uncertainty is assumed to be large and the probability of the eventual outcome exceeding the official estimate is greater than 50%. (In other words, it is more likely that the CEGB have underestimated rather than over-estimated capital costs.) Similar asymmetric distributions for AGR and coal plant capital costs are adopted. These are our subjective views – others may wish to represent uncertainty in a different way regarding both the shape of the distributions chosen and the overall ranges of uncertainty considered.

For fuel costs the important indicator is the real per cent per annum increase in the cost of fuel to the utility. We again adopt a triangular distribution to represent uncertainty in this rate of increase for both coal and nuclear fuel costs (because of the similarity between PWR and AGR fuel – both use uranium in the dioxide form enriched to around 3% – a single distribution is used to represent fuel-cost escalation for both reactor types). As with capital costs, the range of the distributions is wide (reflecting lessons learnt from the oil market during the 1970s) and, for

Table 7.1 *Uncertain variables and subjective probability distributions*

Uncertain variables		Units	Triangular probability distribution		
			Lower limit *L*	Mode *M*	Upper limit *U*
Capital costs	Coal	1982 £/kW	581	830	1660
	Oil	(including	519	742	1484
	AGR	interest during	1208	1726	3452
	PWR	construction)	988	1411	2822
Fuel costs	Coal	% per annum	−1	1.7	3
	Oil	increase above	−1	1.5	3
	Nuclear	1981 levels	0	1.5	4
Availabilities	Coal	percentage points	−15	0	15
	Oil	change from base	−15	0	15
	AGR	case values	−15	0	15
	PWR		−15	0	15

the case of nuclear fuel, the mode of the distribution is not based on the CEGB's view of the future, but relies on a less optimistic view of overall nuclear fuel cycle costs (the CEGB adopt a 1% per annum real increase whereas we choose a value of 1.5% per annum for the mode).

Plant availabilities are the last set of variables which are likely to have a major impact on the selection of the most economic type of baseload plant. Here the simple approach of using a symmetric triangular distribution to represent variations from some central view of plant availabilities[15] is adopted, with the upper and lower bounds of the distribution being 15 percentage points above and below this central view respectively.

The distributions chosen to represent what we see as the high degree of uncertainty surrounding future values of capital costs, fuel costs and plant availabilities are summarised in table 7.1. These distributions represent our subjective opinions, and alternative views of the future will inevitably exist (it should be clear by now that the CEGB would probably not choose to admit such a wide range of uncertainty as we feel is prudent).

We have also included data on capital costs, fuel costs and availabilities of oil-fired plant in table 7.1, in addition to information on the three principal options of coal, AGR and PWR. The CEGB have completely rejected oil-fired stations for baseload generation because of their unfavourable economics. By explicitly including them as a fourth option for new plant construction, we are able to assess whether the CEGB's rejection of this plant type was justified.

Table 7.2 *Results of incorporating uncertainty into investment appraisal*

Plant type	Probability of plant representing the least-cost option for baseload operation
PWR	60%
Coal	27%
AGR	10%
Oil	3%

Having selected probability distributions for the key uncertain variables, it is necessary to incorporate this uncertainty into our LP model of the supply system. This is done by sampling values for each of the variables from our probability distributions and running the model a large number of times, using different values for the variables in each run.[16] In this way we determine the likelihood of a given type of plant representing the least cost option simply by observing in what proportion of LP runs it is chosen to provide baseload generation in preference to its competitors.

The results of this analysis are presented in table 7.2. Two points are immediately obvious: (a) PWRs appear as the most probable least-cost option and (b) it is unlikely that oil-fired plant will prove economic for baseload generation. At first sight these results would appear to support the CEGB view that PWR construction should start at the earliest opportunity, and no consideration need be given to oil plant. We would argue, however, that the results have a much more important and far-reaching interpretation and may actually help to explain the generally low estimates of future installed nuclear capacity that we presented in Chapter 2.

We started our account of the problems which nuclear power faces by contrasting, in Chapter 1, an early 1970s view of nuclear reactor economics with the situation as seen a decade later. The picture we painted was one in which the economic scales appeared to be tipped heavily in favour of nuclear power just ten years ago but have now swung to a position of balance, or at least one in which the outcome is, in many countries, unresolved. Our mathematical analysis of the situation in the UK, using our own subjective opinions on a whole range of uncertain variables, has helped confirm our earlier view. Readers with views similar to our own should also now have no intellectual difficulty admitting that nuclear power is not *certain* to represent the most economic option.

The PWR still appears to be the best bet for power generation but its position is no longer unassailable. On our assumptions, there is just a

60% chance that it will prove economically optimal, and coal, as the next closest competitor, has a 27% chance of becoming the least-cost option. The problem arises as to what happens in the 40% of cases in which PWR loses the economic advantage.

Utility planners worldwide can look to a number of cases in which the outcome of a nuclear project, started amidst a mood of great optimism, is now seen to have been not marginally uneconomic, but an unmitigated commercial disaster. Several examples of such projects were discussed in the country profiles of Chapter 2 and included schemes such as the WPPSS plants in the US, the first UK AGRs (particularly Dungeness B), and the Zwentendorf reactor in Austria.

Against this background, the economic advantage of nuclear power (PWRs and AGRs in our analysis) is seen by many planners to be insufficiently compelling to embark on a major programme of nuclear expansion. The problem is further exacerbated by the downturn in electricity demand growth experienced throughout the OECD countries in the late 1970s and early 1980s. This has enabled the options of delaying decisions, or constructing modest amounts of conventional thermal plant, to be given serious consideration.

In the present climate it now seems unlikely that countries will embark on nuclear programmes on anything like the scale of that undertaken by France in the early 1970s. This does not mean, however, that no nuclear construction will take place, and in the next chapter we outline a not uncommon situation in which nuclear power economics may still appear extremely attractive.

8

The economics of enabling decisions

The financial risks of embarking on a major programme of nuclear expansion now appear too great for many countries, even though nuclear power still appears to have the edge over coal, its closest rival, in a majority of situations. During the rest of the 1980s it now seems unlikely that any countries, at least in the Western world, will embark on a nuclear programme anything like as large as that chosen by France in the early 1970s. In some countries nuclear moratoria (either *de facto* or *de jure*) will continue, but in others the nuclear option will remain open and a modest amount of nuclear construction will probably take place. This is because of the favourable economics of what we call enabling decisions.

In this context we define a positive enabling decision to be the construction of one (or perhaps two or three) nuclear units, not just to produce low-cost electricity (for, as we have seen in Chapter 7, it is far from certain that such an outcome will be forthcoming), but to maintain the option of employing nuclear technology in the future. The decision to make a limited commitment to nuclear power is important as it 'enables' the nuclear option to be pursued with vigour in the event that the economics, as determined by the single plant (or small number of plants), prove to be favourable.

This chapter is taken up with a detailed examination of a specific enabling decision. Again we concentrate on the electricity supply system in England and Wales, where the CEGB is responsible for power generation and bulk transmission, and we build on the analysis of the previous chapter. However, decisions of this type will be taken in several Western countries in the period up to 1990, as should be clear from Chapter 2, and the methodology presented here provides a suitable framework for analysing each of these decisions.

121

Sizewell B as an enabling decision

The CEGB is one of the world's largest fully integrated power utilities (along with EDF of France), operating approximately 55 GW of generating plant. In the financial year 1982/3 around 80% of total generation was met by coal-fired plant, with nuclear power meeting 14% of demand. At present, in mid-1983, eight first-generation Magnox stations are in operation along with one AGR. Three more AGRs are on the point of entering service and a further similar station is under construction.

The Magnox reactor is an obsolete design and, because of the many problems with the AGR concept (described in Chapter 2), the CEGB now wish to construct a Westinghouse PWR at Sizewell on the Suffolk coast. This proposal is being examined at a Public Inquiry which started in January 1983 and is scheduled to finish around the middle of 1984. The purpose of the Inquiry is to guide government decision-makers who must decide, in the face of conflicting evidence, whether to give approval to the project.

It is now becoming clear that arguments at the Inquiry will centre on the two key issues of safety and economics. In this chapter, we analyse the economics of Sizewell B, using probabilistic decision analysis, a technique which has been applied successfully to a number of problems in the energy field in recent years.[1-5]

Decision analysis explores in a formal, structured manner, the possible outcome of a particular decision.[6] The consequences of each option are

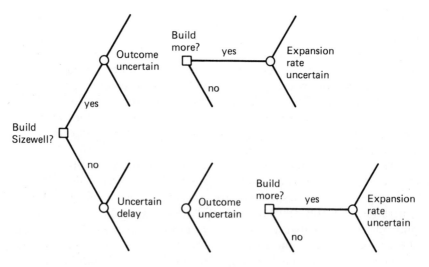

Figure 8.1 Decision tree for the Sizewell B PWR

considered in turn, with probabilities being assigned to events over which the decision-maker has no control. For readers not familiar with decision analysis, a simple example, taken from everyday life, is given in Appendix A.

The decision tree for the economics of Sizewell B is shown in figure 8.1, in which time increases from left to right, decision nodes are represented by squares and chance nodes by circles. If Sizewell B is approved, this may be viewed as an enabling decision, leading to the possibility of the PWR becoming the established UK reactor type. Alternatively, if Sizewell is not approved, the PWR option must effectively be considered closed, at least for some period of time.[7]

If the Sizewell PWR is built (i.e. following the 'yes' branch at the first decision node of figure 8.1), there is a wide range of possibilities regarding the economics of the project ('Outcome uncertain' chance node), but the option of building further PWRs is opened ('Build more?' decision node). If this latter option is taken (and it presumably won't be unless experience with Sizewell is favourable), the rate of future PWR expansion is also uncertain depending, as it does, on electricity demand and plant retirement, as well as on reactor manufacturing capability.

If a decision not to build Sizewell is taken (the 'no' branch of the first decision node), there will be some delay before PWRs can again be considered in the UK. The delay may be long (even infinite) but is, in any event, uncertain. After this delay, PWR construction may take place (if the economics are favourable) and will be subject to similar uncertainties as would be encountered following an initial decision to go ahead with Sizewell.

We wish to calculate the overall economic benefit (which, in this context, may be positive or negative) to the CEGB system of building Sizewell B. To do this we calculate overall system costs for the two possible future paths ('yes' or 'no' at the first decision node). In other words, two runs of our cost-minimising LP of Chapter 7 are required, one with and one without PWRs available at an early date. The difference between the total discounted system costs obtained from the two runs, we call the net decision benefit (NDB).

The NDB is much more than an indicator to be used for choosing between alternative projects.[8] It is a measure of the overall benefit of approving construction of the Sizewell reactor, and takes account not only of the impact of a single PWR but also the effect on the total supply network, through time, of other PWRs which may follow Sizewell if they are justified on economic grounds.

From our discussion in the previous chapter, it should be clear that we would not consider a single calculation of the NDB, in which no account

Table 8.1 *Uncertain variables and subjective probability distributions used in the Sizewell decision analysis* (in addition to those of table 7.1)

Uncertain variables	Units	Triangular probability distributions		
		Lower limit L	Mode M	Upper limit U
Electricity demand	per annum increase post 1981	−1	1	4
Load duration curve shape	ratio of peak to baseload cf. 1981	0.75	1	1.1
Delay for PWR introduction following rejection of Sizewell at Public Inquiry	years	1	10	20
Maximum PWR expansion rate	% per annum up to limit of 20 GW in a five-year period	5	10	20

was taken of uncertainty, to be particularly helpful. We again represent variables such as capital costs, fuel prices and plant availabilities by subjective probability distributions. In addition, there are a number of other variables, not required in our calculation of the least-cost option for baseload plant, which must be included in our NDB calculations.

The variables involved are electricity demand (both the absolute magnitude of demand and the relative split between peak and baseload demand); the delay before PWRs may be introduced if Sizewell is rejected; and the maximum PWR expansion rate possible, if their economics turn out to be favourable, after construction of the first station. These new variables are also uncertain. For each of them we again use triangular probability distributions, the details appearing in table 8.1. For capital costs, fuel costs and availabilities, we continue to use the distributions introduced in the last chapter (see table 7.1). In all cases the distributions chosen are broad, reflecting our subjective view that overall uncertainty is large.

Latin Hypercube Sampling

Theory
We have described the framework within which we wish to

analyse the Sizewell decision, introduced the NDB, and presented probability distributions that quantify the uncertainty surrounding the input
variables. It now remains for us to explain how we calculate an expected
value of the NDB[9] given our views on uncertainty. In other words, we will
provide an outline of the sampling technique alluded to in Chapter 7
which led there to our figure of 60% for the probability that PWRs will be
economic. The description of the sampling scheme used is inevitably
somewhat technical. However, a detailed understanding of the technique
is not essential for an appreciation of the general arguments we are pursuing and some readers may wish to move directly to the description of
the application of the method to a calculation of the NDB.

The technique we use is Latin Hypercube Sampling (LHS),[10] which
offers a convenient way of establishing the extent to which uncertainties
in input data affect the results obtained from a computer model. Briefly,
the method may be described as follows. We wish to study the output (in
this chapter the NDB) of a mathematical model as a function of the inputs
to the model. In particular, both a probability distribution of the output
variable and the sensitivity of this output variable to various inputs are
required. The first step is to select sample values from the distributions
used to represent uncertain input data. Rather than employing systematic
sampling (such as extreme values from a distribution) or completely
random sampling (as in ordinary Monte Carlo studies), Latin Hypercube
Sampling employs a mixture of the two.

We let $x_1, x_2, \ldots, x_I$ be the I input variables. Each x_i has a probability
density function $f_i(x)$ for $x_i^L < x < x_i^H$, which, in our case, is the triangular distribution assumed for each of our uncertain variables. We define
constants $x_i^L = a_{i0} < a_{i1} < \ldots < a_{in} = x_i^H$ such that the probability content of each interval (a_{ij-1}, a_{ij}) is $1/n$. The jth interval of variable i is
denoted by I_j^i. In other words, we have divided the domain of the probability density function of each input variable into n equal probability
intervals, where n will be the total number of computer runs.

As an example, consider the case in which we have three independent
input variables ($i = 1, 2, 3$) and we wish to make eight computer runs.
Each variable is divided into eight intervals ($I_1^i, \ldots, I_8^i$). For each variable,
each interval will appear exactly once, the intervals being randomly per-
muted to determine which will appear in any given computer run. One
possible scheme is illustrated in table 8.2. With intervals for each variable
assigned to a given computer run, it is simply necessary to select randomly
a particular value from each interval and perform the computer run with
these selected input values.

Having performed all our computer runs (eight in the present example),
it is possible to obtain a probability distribution of the output variable

Table 8.2 *An example of intervals to be*
sampled for a LHS design – 3 variables,
8 computer runs

Computer run	Input variables		
	1	2	3
1	I_3	I_7	I_2
2	I_6	I_2	I_1
3	I_1	I_3	I_7
4	I_8	I_6	I_5
5	I_7	I_1	I_8
6	I_2	I_4	I_4
7	I_5	I_8	I_6
8	I_4	I_5	I_3

and so satisfy our first goal of sensitivity analysis. However, we also wish to determine the sensitivity of the output variable to changes in particular inputs and for this we need a sensitivity function. The function we choose is the partial rank correlation coefficient (PRCC).[11] Partial correlation coefficients are designed to measure the degree of linear association between two variables from a set of variables, after adjusting for the effects of other variables in the set. The partial correlation coefficient is therefore superior to the more conventional finite difference ratio, obtained by holding all but one of the input variables fixed at their nominal values and differencing on the extreme values of the free variable. The use of ranked data[12] in the calculation of partial correlation coefficients effects some smoothing of nonlinearities.[13]

In the present analysis, the PRCC for each variable measures the degree of linear association between the variable and the output and lies in the range $-1 \leqslant \text{PRCC} \leqslant 1$. The further from 0 that the PRCC of a variable lies, the greater the impact that variable has on the result.

Application

We explicitly include uncertainty in 15 input variables when calculating the NDB of Sizewell B: the 11 variables associated with capital costs, fuel costs and plant availabilities, presented in table 7.1, along with our 4 additional variables of table 8.1. Other input variables necessary for running the LP model, which are not included in either table 7.1 or table 8.1, may also be uncertain. However, we do not explicitly include them in the sensitivity analysis as we feel that their influence on the value of the NDB is, in most cases, likely to be small. Variables associated with generating plant, such as gas turbine and pumped storage, not used for baseload generation and installed in relatively small quantities, fall into this category. In addition, a single value of 5% is used throughout for the discount rate (the required rate of return set by Government for major public sector projects in the UK). We do not consider uncertainty in this variable, which has been changed twice within the last ten years, not because its effect is small but because of its correlation with other variables, particularly coal costs.[14] Uncertainties in plant lifetimes are also excluded because, within plausible ranges of between, say, 25 to 35 years, plant lifetimes have been shown to have little impact on this type of investment appraisal due to the effect of using a positive discount rate.[15]

The LHS technique requires that all uncertain input variables are independent. For most variables this is unlikely to cause any difficulty. For others, particularly coal and oil fuel costs, and coal and nuclear capital costs, this assumption requires some justification.

Within the timespan of this study (to 2020), it is considered likely that the price of oil will continue to exhibit sharp rises, during periods when the small number of producer countries are able to extract considerable monopoly profits, followed by a fall of price in real (and even monetary) terms. An increase in world coal trade will prevent world coal prices following the oil price upwards, with a significant number of large producers being active in the market and coal prices being dictated by marginal production costs.

As far as capital costs are concerned, it may reasonably be argued that coal and nuclear construction costs would be highly correlated as both types of station require similar skills and technologies (and are frequently built by the same companies). However, recent experience in the UK has indicated that it is not the steady real rise of coal plant construction costs which causes most concern, but the possibility that costs will escalate beyond all reasonable expectations, as happened at the Dungeness B AGR, due to a combination of factors from poor project management to gross deficiencies in the original design work. For this reason we argue, not only that coal and nuclear capital costs, for example, are independent, but that such an assumption is essential if the possibility of particularly poor (or particularly good) achievement at construction sites in the future is to be included in the analysis.

The final step in the application of the LHS technique to the Sizewell problem is the choice of the number of pairs of computer runs to be performed (1 pair for each value of the NDB). This is dictated by the trade-off between obtaining statistically significant PRCCs and limiting the use of computer resources. The purpose of the sensitivity functions is to determine which input variables have a significant impact on the result,

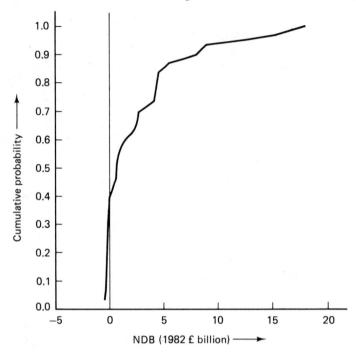

Figure 8.2 Cumulative probability distribution for net decision benefit (NDB)

and for this reason it is necessary to know at what level a PRCC may be considered to be significant. We use 30 pairs of computer runs in the present analysis. For this number of runs and 15 uncertain variables, any PRCC lying outside the range -0.4 to $+0.4$ is significant at the 95% level on a two-tailed test.[16]

The benefit of Sizewell B

Probability distribution

The cumulative probability distribution of the economic benefits obtained from approval of Sizewell B (i.e. the NDB) is shown in figure 8.2. The salient points may be summarised as follows, with all monetary units being 1982 £, discounted to mid-1983.

- The probability of Sizewell leading to a positive benefit is 60%.
- If the benefit is negative (with 40% probability), it will lie in the range zero to $-£422$ million with an expected (mean) value of $-£263$ million.

- If the benefit is positive it will lie in the range zero to £17,821 million with an expected value of £4617 million.
- If Sizewell is built, the overall expected value of the benefit is £2665 million.

These results may also be explained qualitatively. The 60% probability of Sizewell leading to a positive benefit is the result obtained in the previous chapter. We have used distributions for capital and fuel costs and availabilities for Sizewell and its coal, oil and AGR competitors identical to those we adopted in Chapter 7. Once again we come to the conclusion that if a PWR is built, positive benefits are likely but far from certain.

The size of the dis-benefit is relatively small in the 40% of cases in which Sizewell does not prove to be justified on economic grounds, because under these conditions, only one nuclear station is built. Further nuclear construction does not take place as it is assumed that signals concerning the adverse outcome of the Sizewell project will be received in sufficient time to halt further nuclear ordering. What happens, however, if a commitment to additional PWRs is made before it is clear whether Sizewell is justified on economic grounds?

In this case, under conditions adverse to PWR development, two or possibly three uneconomic PWRs would be built rather than the single station (Sizewell) assumed in our analysis. This would have no effect on the likelihood of a negative NDB, but it would increase the absolute magnitude of the NDB in the 40% of cases in which it was negative (and would therefore reduce the overall expected benefit). If it is assumed that a minimum of three PWRs are built rather than one, the costs (negative benefits) will approximately triple in the 40% of cases unfavourable to PWRs. The expected value of the costs will, however, remain much lower than the expected value of the benefits and the overall conclusions from the decision analysis will remain unchanged.

These arguments do not hold for a major programme comprising 10 to 20 PWRs, say, on which construction of all units starts within a short period of perhaps five years. If the PWR proved to be uneconomic in this situation, and the probability of such an occurrence is still 40%, the extra costs incurred may be very large. This again reinforces the conclusions of the previous chapter; PWR economics are such that, although probably favourable, utilities are understandably reluctant to embark on a massive programme.

Our analysis indicates that in the 60% of cases in which a positive NDB is obtained, benefits are potentially very large. This is because Sizewell is a PWR enabling decision. For example, if nuclear capital costs turn out to be lower than expected, coal prices rise significantly and electricity demand increases steadily, then PWR economics become extremely

Table 8.3 *Sensitivity functions (PRCCs)*

Variable no.	Variable		PRCC
1	Coal	⎫	0.475
2	Oil	Capital	−0.003
3	AGR	costs	0.303
4	PWR	⎭	−0.897
5	Coal	⎫	0.693
6	Oil	Fuel	0.098
7	Nuclear	costs	−0.502
8	Demand		0.365
9	LDC shape		−0.267
10	Coal	⎫	−0.395
11	Oil	Availabilities	−0.013
12	AGR		−0.269
13	PWR	⎭	0.498
14	Delay		0.220
15	PWR growth rate		−0.243

favourable and a large programme of PWRs is desirable. Such a programme may only be implemented if the initial decision is taken to
approve the building of Sizewell.

The sensitive variables
The PRCCs of the 15 uncertain variables are given in table 8.3,
from which five variables may be seen to be significant at the 95% level
(their PRCCs lie outside the range −0.4 to +0.4). In decreasing order of
importance these variables are:
1. PWR capital costs
2. Coal price
3. Nuclear fuel cost
4. PWR availability
5. Coal plant capital costs
A negative sign for the PRCC of a variable indicates that the NDB
decreases with an increase in the value of the variable, and vice versa. An
increase in PWR generation costs reduces the value of the NDB and,
therefore, leads to negative values for the PRCCs of PWR capital costs
and nuclear fuel costs, and a positive value for the PRCC of PWR
availability (lower PWR availability means a lower value for the NDB).
Similarly, increases in coal generation costs improve the NDB further
(coal-fired plant is the PWR's closest competitor), and leads to positive
values for the PRCCs of both fuel and capital costs of coal plant.

In addition to the five most significant variables, coal plant availability and electricity demand are significant at the 90% level. None of the variables related to oil-fired plant are significant, reflecting the fact that oil is unlikely to make more than a modest contribution to electricity supply in the future, even with over 10 GW of modern oil-fired plant in service or about to be commissioned on the CEGB system.[17] A further variable included in the analysis but found to be insignificant is the shape of the annual load duration curve.[18] This is particularly noteworthy as one report dealing with the economics of Sizewell placed a great deal of emphasis on this parameter.[19]

Our results show that the debate surrounding the economic prospects for Sizewell should focus principally on PWR construction costs and the future price of coal, with the future demand for electricity, up to now widely considered to be of major importance, being less significant than several other parameters. Also, the attention given by some workers to the worldwide performance of operating PWRs[20] appears justified given the importance of PWR availabilities.

Policy implications

We feel that the analysis presented in this chapter has some important policy implications, as it provides a clear guide for decision-makers faced with conflicting evidence and an uncertain future. As far as the economic assessment of the Sizewell reactor is concerned, the project should be approved even though positive benefits are far from guaranteed.

Many countries now have to decide whether to begin construction of their first nuclear power station. In the UK, opening the PWR option appears to make economic sense, even with competition from indigenous coal and a home-grown nuclear technology (the AGR). In other countries without these competing options such enabling decisions may appear even more attractive. On the other hand, a few countries, such as Egypt, are still contemplating embarking on a major programme of nuclear expansion. The results of our analysis caution against such a strategy in a world in which uncertainty is large and the perception of nuclear power economics has changed dramatically over the last decade.

Appendix A

Decision Analysis – a simple example

As a brief introduction for readers not familiar with the use of decision analysis techniques, consider the following simple example.

On leaving the house in the morning, the schoolteacher must decide whether to take an umbrella. There are two options available – take the umbrella or leave it at home. If it rains and the umbrella was taken, all well and good, but if it remains fine, our hero is unnecessarily burdened with an unwanted umbrella. Similarly, if the umbrella is left at home and the sun shines all day so much the better, but if it were to rain – disaster, particularly if the outcome meant sitting all day in wet clothes! The situation may be represented by the decision tree of figure A.1, in which squares represent decision nodes (over which the decision-maker has control) and circles are chance nodes (outside the decision-makers sphere of influence). Time increases from left to right.

So should the teacher take the umbrella? The answer depends both on the likelihood of it raining and the way in which the four possible outcomes are valued by the decision-maker. We label these four outcomes U_1 to U_4 and assume that P_1 is the probability of having rain, so that $(1 - P_1)$ is the probability of the weather remaining fine.

Let us now assume that the umbrella is left at home. The overall expected value of the outcome is simply given by the summation over all possible events of probability $\times$ outcome. In this case it is $P_1U_3 + (1 - P_1)U_4$. Similarly, the expected value of the outcome if the umbrella is taken is $P_1U_1 + (1 - P_1)U_2$. This leads us directly to a decision-rule; the umbrella should be taken if:

$$P_1U_1 + (1 - P_1)U_2 > P_1U_3 + (1 - P_1)U_4.$$

We have said nothing of how values may be assigned to the four possible outcomes. For completeness a general discussion on utility theory should

132

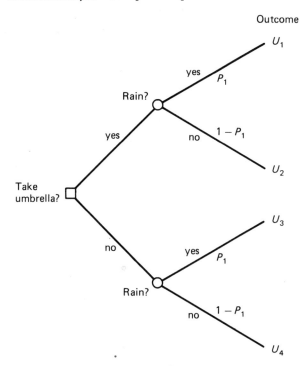

Outcome

Figure A.1 The umbrella decision tree

follow, such as that introducing Von Neumann and Morgenstern's classic text.[21] In this brief description it will suffice to ask the reader to accept that U_4 would be preferred as an outcome to U_3 and that, on a linear scale from 0 to 10, plausible values for the four outcomes might be: $U_1 = 6$; $U_2 = 4$; $U_3 = 0$; $U_4 = 10$ which leads to a decision to carry the umbrella if the probability of rain exceeds 0.5. These values are purely subjective – for example, some people might place U_2 higher than U_1 on our scale, particularly if the umbrella had a possible use in addition to providing protection from the rain (e.g. as a walking stick).

As a final point we would like to discuss briefly uncertainty and the value of additional information. In our present problem uncertainty enters because we do not know whether the rain will take the form of light showers or violent storms, and this will affect our utility values. However, additional information about the risks of rain may be available simply by listening to the weather forecast (and in practice this is how decisions concerning problems of this type are taken – by switching on the radio!). In more complex decision analysis problems, additional information is only available on payment of a fee. Part of the problem is then to decide whether to pay the fee and, a related question, to estimate the value of *perfect* information. (The reference in note 6 deals with the problem in detail.) In the Sizewell decision discussed in the main text, one of the ways of finding out whether PWR economics are favourable is to build one and see. The cost may be thought of as a fee payable for obtaining further information.

9

Trade in nuclear electricity

We described in Chapter 2 the pattern of nuclear generating capacity that we expect to develop to the turn of the century in the world outside communist areas (WOCA). We also indicated that our capacity figures were significantly lower than previous estimates. However, a comparison of aggregate figures masks the full extent of the downturn in forecasts of nuclear penetration which has taken place in just a few years. For example, a report prepared in 1975,[1] just eight years prior to the estimates we made in Chapter 2, showed a rapid expansion of nuclear capacity in all OECD[2] countries, sixteen of which were forecast to have in excess of 10 GW of nuclear capacity by the end of the century. Both Canada and the UK were expected to have 115 GW of nuclear plant in the year 2000, whereas our high estimates for the same year are 23 and 17 GW respectively; 1000 GW of nuclear capacity was confidently predicted for the USA, in comparison with our high figure (which we are far from confident will actually be reached) of 180 GW by the year 2000.

We now believe only eight countries in the whole of WOCA are likely to have more than 10 GW of nuclear plant by the turn of the century (as indicated by our estimates of table 2.2), and of these only six will maintain a steady growth in capacity of at least 5% per annum over the next twenty years. These six countries are listed in table 9.1.

Some of the more significant omissions from table 9.1 are the USA, UK, Sweden and Italy. The estimates for year 2000 capacity made in 1975 for the first two have already been mentioned; a similar estimate for Sweden was 24 GW, while Italy was attributed with a staggering figure of 140 GW (compared with our range of 7–12 GW). In the mid-1970s, predicting the likely takeoff of nuclear power in a country was thought to be a fairly straightforward business. Heavy reliance on expensive fossil fuel, a large integrated electricity grid, and access to advanced technological skills were expected to be necessary and sufficient conditions for a swift buildup of nuclear power capacity. These conditions for rapid nuclear

Table 9.1 *Countries with rapidly growing nuclear capacity until 2000*

	Capacity in 2000 (GW)	Growth rate in capacity 1982–2000 (% per year)
France	70	6.1
Japan	60	7.0
Germany	28	5.8
Canada	18	5.2
Spain	12.5	10.2
Korea	11	16.2

The 2000 figures are the 'low' end of the ranges from Chapter 2.

expansion are satisfied in each of the four countries mentioned above. Despite this, the progress of nuclear power has, in each case, been slowed dramatically.

One of the major reasons for the downturn was the severe world recession which followed the first oil price rise of 1973, the full extent of which was not appreciated in 1975. The downturn in energy demand growth generally, and electricity growth in particular, along with high levels of inflation (which led to problems in financing large capital-intensive projects such as nuclear power stations) had a profound impact. In addition to the effects of the recession, other factors, such as those we have highlighted in Chapters 3 to 8, have also had an impact.

In the USA, a steady updating of regulatory standards following a major nuclear accident has convinced the electric utilities that the odds against making a profit from nuclear power are too high. The UK has experienced construction overruns and poor performance with its indigenous AGR design. This has led the CEGB to seek to widen its options by building a single PWR – a strategy we analysed, in Chapter 8, as a classic enabling decision. The doubts over the future of nuclear power in Sweden occur despite a successful indigenous reactor design, and can be traced to public apprehension, as indicated by the results of a referendum, the ultimate expression of public involvement in decision-making. Italy, despite its chronic shortage of generating capacity and almost total dependence on imported fossil fuel, has been unable to find acceptable sites for nuclear reactors.

A three-way split of countries is therefore appropriate. Those in table 9.1 are the nuclear 'haves'. Those that do not satisfy the traditional conditions for nuclear development, such as adequate grid size and availability of the necessary technical skills, are the 'have nots'. They include, not only

Table 9.2 *The major nuclear 'haves' (H) and 'won't haves' (WH) in the OECD*

North America	Canada	H
	USA	WH
Western Europe	Austria	WH
	France	H
	Germany	H
	Italy	WH
	Netherlands	WH
	Spain	H
	Sweden	WH
	Switzerland	WH
	UK	WH
Pacific	Japan	H

many developing countries, but also countries such as Norway and Australia which have large alternative energy resources available at low cost (hydro and coal respectively). The third group can best be described as the 'won't haves' and includes the four countries discussed above. They are ready and able to increase rapidly their utilisation of nuclear power; they are not willing.

A regional classification of the major 'haves' and 'won't haves' in Western Europe and North America is given in table 9.2. A fascinating pattern emerges. In most cases a 'won't have' country finds a 'have' nearby. This proximity could allow even a 'won't have' to obtain nuclear-generated electricity, not by employing its own indigenous reactor design or by importing nuclear technology from established reactor vendors, but by importing electricity from a 'have' country where the general climate is more favourable to the exploitation of nuclear power.

The stimulus to trade

There are two possible spurs to persuade neighbouring countries to trade nuclear-generated electricity. The first is a traditional cost advantage. If one of the neighbours can generate nuclear electricity more cheaply than the other; if this cost advantage is great enough to cover any increased transmission charges (including extra power losses); and if the potential importer has no cheaper option available, then a price exists that is high enough to persuade the potential exporter to produce electricity, yet low enough to persuade the potential importer to buy. Trade will occur if it is permitted to do so, and if the cost of electricity supply is the only consideration. This mechanism may stimulate trade between certain 'haves' and 'have nots'.

The second possible spur to trade is provided by our contention that cost is not the only consideration when choosing between alternatives for electricity supply. It is this second spur that may provide the stimulus for trade between 'haves' and 'won't haves'. The fundamental difference between these sets of countries can be traced to their different attitudes to the risks of nuclear power compared to other energy sources. Our use of the word risks here is not limited to risks of death or injury but instead represents the all-embracing risk indices of Chapter 6. A little algebra allows us to demonstrate most precisely the conditions that will be conducive to trade.

Conditions for trade

Suppose we have two neighbouring countries, a 'have' and a 'won't have'. Both have the option of using either nuclear power or coal for baseload electricity generation. Both are concerned only with financial effects and risks when deciding which source of energy to use. Country WH ('won't have') is considering how to supply an extra 1 GWyr of baseload electricity.

The financial benefit from having the electricity available is $\$B_{WH}$, regardless of how it is generated. The costs of generating electricity by coal and nuclear power are $\$CC_{WH}$ and $\$CN_{WH}$ respectively. The risks incurred are considered to be RC_{WH} and RN_{WH} respectively, measured on the utility scale from 0 to 100 as in Chapter 6. Country WH makes its choice between coal and nuclear power by examining the overall utility of generating electricity from each of the sources. The utility of coal-fired generation is

$$UC_{WH} = (B_{WH} - CC_{WH}) - WR_{WH} \times RC_{WH}$$

or, in words, the total utility of coal-fired electricity generation is equal to the net financial benefits, minus a weighting factor times the risks incurred. The weighing factor, WR_{WH}, expresses the number of $ compensation required in country WH just to offset an increase in risks by a single point on the utility scale.[3] Likewise the utility of nuclear generation is

$$UN_{WH} = (B_{WH} - CN_{WH}) - WR_{WH} \times RN_{WH}.$$

Because country WH is a 'won't have' it would choose coal rather than nuclear generation if these are the only options, so $UC_{WH} > UN_{WH}$. This is so even though CC_{WH} may be higher than CN_{WH}; the higher risk for nuclear power combines with a relatively high weighting factor to bring the total utility of nuclear generation below that of coal. But country WH has a third option: to import 1 GWyr of nuclear-generated electricity from its neighbour, country H, a nuclear 'have', at a price of T. The utility of this option is

$$UT_{WH} = (B_{WH} - T) - WR_{WH} \times RT_{WH}$$

where RT_{WH} is the risk imposed on country WH by the generation of nuclear electricity in country H. This may well be considered to be small (or even zero), but we retain the term RT_{WH} for completeness. Country WH will decide to import the electricity if $UT_{WH} > UC_{WH}$; that is, if

$$(B_{WH} - T) - WR_{WH} \times RT_{WH} > (B_{WH} - CC_{WH}) - WR_{WH} \times RC_{WH}$$

which reduces to

$$T < CC_{WH} + WR_{WH} \times (RC_{WH} - RT_{WH}).$$

The right-hand side of this expression gives the maximum price for the traded electricity that will induce country WH to purchase rather than generate by its preferred fuel, coal.

Now consider the potential exporter, country H. If it generates 1 GWyr of nuclear electricity for export it obtains a revenue of T. In so doing it incurs costs of CN_H to generate the electricity and CT_H to transmit it across its national boundary to country WH. It also incurs a risk RN_H from the nuclear generation. The total utility it obtains from the trade is therefore

$$UT_H = (T - CN_H - CT_H) - WR_H \times RN_H$$

where WR_H is the weighting factor applied to risks by country H. The alternative to exporting is simply to refuse to trade, which brings zero revenue, cost and risk and so an overall utility of zero. Country H will be inclined to export if $UT_H > 0$, which requires $T > CN_H + CT_H + WR_H \times RN_H$. This sets the minimum price for the traded electricity that will induce country H to generate nuclear electricity for export. Comparing this with the maximum price that country WH will be willing to pay shows that a potential for trade exists provided

$$CN_H + CT_H + WR_H \times RN_H < CC_{WH} + WR_{WH} \times (RC_{WH} - RT_{WH}).$$

If this condition holds, there exists a price T that will be high enough to induce country H to export, yet low enough to induce country WH to import. Trade would benefit both countries.[4]

A numerical example

Inserting some numerical values can help to illustrate the principles at work. Typical generating costs might be $100 × 10^6$ per GWyr (= ¢1.14 per kWh) for nuclear power and $120 × 10^6$ per GWyr (= ¢1.37 per kWh) for coal-fired generation in country WH. We adopt these values for CN_{WH} and CC_{WH} respectively. We shall assume country WH uses something like the 'C' set of weights from Chapter 6 to combine the risks from electricity generation, and so adopt a value of 60 for RN_{WH}. It also has a slightly less risky coal industry than the example in Chapter 6, giving a value of 40 for RC_{WH}.[5]

What might be an appropriate value for the weight attached to risks, WR_{WH}? Under the 'C' set of weights, an increase in public deaths of 1 per GWyr produces a rise of 2 in the risk index. If each public death is valued at $4 × 10^6$ (a not unreasonable figure), this gives $2 × 10^6$ as the value of WR_{WH}. Adopting this value gives

$$UC_{WH} = (B_{WH} - CC_{WH}) - WR_{WH} × RC_{WH}$$
$$= B_{WH} - (120 + 2.0 × 40) × 10^6$$

$$= B_{WH} - 200 × 10^6,$$

$$UN_{WH} = (B_{WH} - CN_{WH}) - WR_{WH} × RN_{WH}$$
$$= B_{WH} - (100 + 2.0 × 60) × 10^6$$

$$= B_{WH} - 220 × 10^6.$$

Therefore $UC_{WH} > UN_{WH}$ and so country WH adopts coal-fired rather than nuclear electricity generation despite the lower costs of nuclear power. It is a 'won't have' country.

Let us assume that country H has slightly lower generating costs for nuclear power than country WH, $90 × 10^6$ per GWyr (¢1.0 per kWh), due perhaps to series ordering of identical reactors. This is the value of CN_H. The cost of transmitting nuclear electricity from country H to WH adds $40 × 10^6$ per GWyr to the cost. This is the value of CT_H. So the total cost incurred by country H in generating nuclear electricity for export to country WH is $130 × 10^6$ per GWyr, higher than the cost of electricity generation with either nuclear power or coal in country WH. Therefore, in the absence of different views about risks, no incentive for trade would exist. However, country H adopts something like the 'A' set of weights from Chapter 6 and so has a value of 10 for RN_H. With the 'A' set of weights, an increase of 1 public death per year produces a rise in the risk index of 3.3. Let us assume that country H values each public death slightly lower than country WH, at $3.3 × 10^6$. This gives $WR_H = 1 × 10^6$ as the weight attached to risks in country H. Finally, country WH feels it is still exposed to a risk of 10 if it imports nuclear electricity from H, as opposed to 60 if it generates nuclear electricity itself. This is the value we use for RT_{WH}.

Now we are able to calculate whether the potential for trade exists. The minimum price for traded electricity that is acceptable to country H is

$$CN_H + CT_H + WR_H \times RN_H = (90 + 40 + 10) \times 10^6$$
$$= 140 \times 10^6.$$

This is required to pay for the financial costs and compensate country H for running the risks of nuclear generation.

The maximum price that country WH will be willing to pay is

$$CC_{WH} + WR_{WH} \times (RC_{WH} - RT_{WH}) = (120 + 2.0 \times 30) \times 10^6$$
$$= 180 \times 10^6.$$

Therefore, in our example, there is a potential for country H to export nuclear electricity to country WH at a price of between \$140 and \$180 $\times 10^6$ per GWyr (¢1.6 and ¢2.05 per kWh). This trade would be to the benefit of both countries.

If the trade occurs, country WH is essentially paying country H to bear risks that its own population has decided not to accept. Some might feel that there is something slightly immoral in this arrangement. To our mind, the trade is almost guaranteed to be fair. No one is coercing country H into exporting. Country WH must be willing to pay quite a substantial premium to avoid running a risk that country H views as small. No wonder country H is happy to oblige. It is rather as though a rich old man were prepared to pay you a large sum to cross a main road and collect his prescription. You view the risk as trivial; he does not. Of course you still have to settle on a fee for your services, and our formulation of the problem merely sets bounds upon what the fee can be if the transaction is to be mutually beneficial, and so stand a chance of taking place. We would just note that if a number of able-bodied young people are queueing up to assist the old man, it would be wise not to demand an unreasonably high fee to perform, what is after all, a simple task.

Similarly for the case of electricity trade. If H is the only country prepared to export nuclear-generated electricity, there is little to stop it demanding close to the maximum that country WH would be prepared to pay. On the other hand, if a large number of exporters are offering electricity to WH, it would be wise for country H to agree a price close to the minimum acceptable, assuming that no possibility exists for cartel action.

France and the UK

The contrasting fortunes of the French and British nuclear industries provide a second example of a potential for trade. A recent report[6] indicates that construction costs for French PWRs are less than 50% of those anticipated for Sizewell B in the UK, a cost advantage which translates into lower prices for nuclear electricity in France. Costs for DC transmission links across the Channel are such that even when they are added to the generation costs of French reactors, nuclear electricity generated in France for UK use still enjoys an appreciable cost advantage over electricity generated by a PWR at Sizewell.

Identifying France with country H and the UK with country WH, the figures translate into 160×10^6 per GWyr for CN_H, 80×10^6 per GWyr for CT_H, and 345×10^6 per GWyr for CN_{WH}.[7] By its application to build Sizewell B, the CEGB has shown that it believes the cost of coal-fired generation, CC_{WH}, to be higher still. A clear potential for trade exists, since $CN_H + CT_H$ is lower than the cheapest domestic alternative available to the CEGB. Exports of electricity from France to the UK at a price of between $240 and 345×10^6 per GWyr (¢2.7 and ¢3.9 per kWh) would be to the benefit of both countries.

We have not mentioned different attitudes to risk in this second example. The case for trading nuclear electricity between France and the UK appears at first sight to be based on a straightforward cost advantage. This cost advantage derives from two sources. Firstly the economies that come from large-scale ordering of a settled reactor design in France compare favourably with the decision in the UK to apply initially for permission to build a single PWR. Secondly, the French reactor designs do not contain some of the additional safety features that have been demanded in the UK. It is impossible to say at present how much of the cost advantage comes from each source. The extra safety measures at the Sizewell PWR have added at least 10% to the cost of that design,[8] and are likely to lengthen the construction time, indicating that the second source of cost differences cannot be dismissed as being negligible. So even if the incentive to trade appears to have nothing to do with different attitudes to risk, it may be that these attitudes contribute significantly, at an underlying level, to different nuclear generation costs in the two countries.

Further examples

Further possibilities for nuclear trade exist, as table 9.2 clearly shows, two of which we highlight here. The first is the case of France and Italy. Italy is currently facing severe problems of undercapacity of generating plant caused largely by difficulties in obtaining suitable sites for nuclear plant because of strong local opposition. Here Italy is clearly a 'won't have' country in which WR_{WH}, the weighting factor associated with nuclear risks, is much higher than WR_H, the risk weighting factor prevailing in France. In addition, with CN_H being much lower than CN_{WH}, and CC_{WH} also being high because of a lack of indigenous fossil fuels and siting difficulties, which also apply to coal stations, our necessary condition for trade to take place is easily satisfied. The fact that such trade is actually taking place, as discussed in Chapter 2, lends weight to these somewhat abstract arguments.

The second example is that of the USA and Canada. As we have seen, the USA has become a classic 'won't have' country in which both the scores on our risk index of Chapter 6, particularly regarding unknown risk and dread risk, and the risk weighting factor, WR_{WH}, appearing in our overall expression of utility, attract high values. In addition nuclear costs in the USA, CN_{WH}, are now probably higher than in any country in the world. Canada, on the other hand, while not enjoying the very low nuclear generation costs of the French, does have a unique reactor technology which, it believes, may become a world-beater in the 1990s if nuclear ordering recovers from current low levels. Electricity demand in Canada itself is insufficient to justify the large programme of Candu reactors necessary to establish the system as a leading contender in world markets. This explains why attention has been turned to the enormous energy market of the Northern US: a market in which home-grown nuclear power no longer competes, and significant quantities of high-cost oil and gas (the resource cost of which is high even if the actual price charged is low) are still used for power generation. Once again, our necessary condition for trade is satisfied; time will tell if such trade develops.

Barriers to trade

We have kept our formulation as simple as possible in this chapter to bring out clearly two basic reasons for trading nuclear electricity: a cost advantage or a different attitude to risks. There are several factors we have so far omitted that might restrain trade even in those cases where it looks to be mutually beneficial. We briefly consider four possible barriers.

The first is technological. If it were impossible or prohibitively expensive to transmit electricity between countries then no trade would occur. But it does not look as though this will be a serious barrier. The advantages offered to most developed countries by large integrated grids have led to the development of very efficient and cost-effective methods of transmission over long distances. The 2 GW link between France and the

UK, currently under construction and due for completion in 1986, shows that large-scale under-sea transmission is technically feasible. Differing standard voltages and frequencies in importer and exporter countries present little difficulty with the use of transformers and AC–DC–AC links. All in all, the technology to permit trade is readily available.

The second possible barrier is political. Countries may be unwilling to import from neighbours of a markedly different political complexion for fear of providing a lever that could upset the balance on broader issues. However, this does not look to be a problem for two reasons: All the trades that are suggested by table 9.2 would be between countries that are close politically as well as geographically. Even if this were not so, several examples of existing international energy trade demonstrate that huge political barriers can be overcome or sidestepped if the economic incentive is there. We are thinking particularly of the gas pipeline from the USSR to Western Europe and the proposal for UK companies to aid China in its search for oil. Even the heavy reliance of most of the Western world on oil from the Middle East involves trade between countries much further apart politically than any of our potential nuclear trading neighbours.

Thirdly, we have suggested that either a cost advantage or a different view of risks will provide the incentive to trade. But countries do have other concerns, one of which is a strong desire for security of supply. Imported oil or gas may in some circumstances not be totally secure; exporters have been known to curtail supplies or demand higher prices. However, oil and gas can be easily stored. The USA is building up a strategic petroleum reserve, capable of meeting total national demand for 90 days, which is to be drawn upon in times of supply disruption. There is, at present, no possibility of building up a 'strategic reserve of electricity', and long-term electricity storage will not be a viable option, for both technical and economic reasons, in the foreseeable future.

It therefore seems likely that if large-scale trade does occur, the importing country will have to rely on the exporter to maintain security of supply. Incorporating severe financial penalties for failing to deliver electricity on demand into supply contracts may help to alleviate the problem. Whether this would be acceptable to importing countries that have traditionally placed great emphasis on maintenance of supply from the generating sector remains to be seen. Rational debate on the matter would have to start with a detailed examination of the likelihood of the exporting country failing to meet its obligations, compared to the rate of supply disruption from strikes and other domestic causes.[9] Considerable mutual cooperation and exchange of power currently takes place between the countries of Western Europe, largely through the auspices of the UCPTE and Nordel[10] cooperative groups. Within these groups some countries such as West Germany and Denmark even now emerge as substantial net importers of electricity.

The fourth possible barrier to trade is potentially the most serious, not at present but in the future. What happens if there is another accident, similar to or worse than TMI? We have suggested that a major stimulus to trade could well come from differing views of the risks from nuclear power. Even if the stimulus is superficially a straightforward cost advantage, we have to ask how that cost advantage comes about. All advanced countries have identical light water reactor technology available through licensing arrangements; all have the requisite skills to build nuclear stations and enough suitable sites on which to place them. We might then expect any cost advantage to be small, except for the different safety standards that potential trading partners demand.

One possible rationale for retaining confidence in the safety of existing PWR designs is a feeling that the accident at TMI was nothing more than an unlucky coincidence, and that the overall frequency of nuclear core meltdowns is close to the low figure calculated by the WASH-1400 probability risk assessment. We saw in Chapter 3 that at present this requires a large degree of faith in the judgement of the analytical modellers, but as time goes by and more electricity is generated, the story told by operating experience will once more come into line with the meltdown frequencies of WASH-1400, provided no more core meltdowns occur. We saw that, on our projections of Chapter 2, by 1985 the 5% lower limit on core meltdown frequency will drop to the same figure as the 95% upper limit of WASH-1400, 3×10^{-4} meltdowns per reactor year. By this time it will at least be possible to say that the error bars around the core meltdown estimates of judgement and experience overlap. Those determined to retain faith in the PRA studies will be able to do so. However if another core meltdown occurs in the near future it will be difficult for even the most phlegmatic observer to retain a belief in the PRA results, given the steadily mounting evidence that they understate the risks. In Chapter 5 we expressed our opinion that reactions to another nuclear accident may be severe enough to force operators to close down similar stations in their country. If this should happen, it is difficult to imagine any concerned citizen taking the view that risks are small enough to allow trade in nuclear electricity to commence or continue. This reassessment of the risks by potential exporters may be the most serious threat to traded nuclear electricity that could occur, since it would remove at a stroke one major underlying reason for trade to be contemplated: the different view of risks that 'haves' and 'won't haves' adopt.

10

Some pointers to the future

We have covered a lot of ground since our attempt in Chapter 1 to recapture the professional optimism about nuclear prospects that existed in the mid-1970s. Chapters 3 to 9 had two aims: to shed some light on why this optimism has been so widely replaced by a sense of uncertainty and doubt; and to indicate how decisions can be taken even in this climate.

The analysis of Chapter 3 demonstrated that operating experience with light water reactors no longer supports the very low frequencies of nuclear core meltdowns predicted by almost all the probabilistic risk assessments since the pioneering work of Rasmussen in 1975. The realisation that this report and all subsequent studies could have seriously underestimated the risk of a meltdown has naturally produced or maintained considerable anxiety amongst those who take an interest in nuclear matters.

We incorporated anxiety into a total risk index for nuclear power and other energy sources in Chapter 6. The results indicated that the risks from nuclear power could be greater or less than those from competing technologies, depending on the relative weights given to avoiding anxiety or saving lives.

We found in Chapter 4 that following the accident at Three Mile Island a statistically significant fall in the load factors of pressurised water reactors occurred throughout the world. Other reactor types were unaffected. So reactor accidents can have global consequences for operators of nuclear power stations. The effect of this can be expressed as a surcharge on the capital cost of each new station, to cover the possibility of having to respond to an accident anywhere in the world. All other things equal, this surcharge increases with the worldwide use of a reactor type. Making plausible numerical assumptions we demonstrated in Chapter 5 that the surcharge on a PWR may exceed that on a lesser-used design by several per cent of the capital cost. Companies wanting to

146

operate nuclear power stations would be wise to take the accident surcharge into account when deciding which reactor type to use.

In Chapter 7 we inserted early 1980s parameters into our model of power station choice to show that even the economic benefits of nuclear power stations no longer look certain. The principle cause of this has been the escalation of nuclear station capital costs since the 1970s. The main effect has been to sow seeds of doubt about the wisdom of committing large sums to a nuclear station construction programme. However, many countries are not yet in the position of having to decide upon a large programme. Instead, they have to decide whether to build one, or a small number, of reactors to keep the nuclear option open. The economic assessment of this type of enabling decision was performed in Chapter 8. Even when the country already has its own indigenous but expensive reactor design, it seems the benefits from keeping options open far outweigh the costs. For countries approaching nuclear power for the first time, the economics of an enabling decision look even better.

In Chapter 9 we derived the conditions under which even those countries which won't have nuclear reactors in their power supply systems could still obtain nuclear-generated electricity – by importing it from a neighbouring country in which the climate of opinion is less hostile towards nuclear power. We identified the stimulus to trade as either a straightforward cost advantage or a difference in attitude towards the risks of nuclear power. Even when the stimulus appears to be the former, the latter may be a major underlying reason for the cost advantage to exist.

Diagnosing nuclear health

This brief résumé of the material covered in earlier chapters helps to show why many earlier forecasts of rapid nuclear power growth have been proved over-optimistic. We can now see that the health of the nuclear industry in any country will be affected by many factors in addition to the economic and safety advantages claimed for nuclear power in Chapter 1.

A centrally controlled, technocratic decision-making structure would probably favour reliance on the 'A' set of risk weights of Chapter 6 which support nuclear power. Proponents of the 'C' set of weights might be ignored or persuaded by financial inducements. By contrast, a political system in which energy sector decision-making received major inputs from regionally devolved legislative assemblies, may be more influenced by public anxieties at grassroots level, and hence more likely to adopt the 'C' set of weights. In some of this latter group of countries, the nuclear industry might be able to secure its survival by vigorously applying some of the more promising risk-reduction activities described in Chapter 6. In others, nuclear power proponents may have been protected from the harsh necessity of selling themselves to the public for so long that they would find it impossible to make the required adjustments. Their industry might succumb to the contagious disease of public hostility.

In addition to the traditional influences, we have identified two other factors determining the odds against an economic payoff from a programme of nuclear reactors. Firstly, if designs are constantly modified and new safety features incorporated, the capital cost of nuclear stations will be continually escalating and the probability of profitable operation diminishing. A considerable advantage may be enjoyed in those countries where a settled design can be supplied 'off-the-shelf'. The conclusions of Chapter 6 suggest that the extra cost of additional safety features would have only a negligible effect on the total risk, unless the off-the-shelf design was seen as recklessly dangerous.

Secondly, incorporating our accident surcharge of Chapter 5 into the economic calculations might also be enough to tip the balance against a nuclear programme in those countries using a common reactor type. Some reduction of the surcharge could be achieved by successfully marketing the reactor as a unique national standard, or by achieving such a large market share that a shutdown became unthinkable. Countries that adopted a less common design would otherwise enjoy a lower accident surcharge.

If a case could be made for obtaining further information, it is almost certain that an enabling decision to build a small number of nuclear stations would be economically justified. The enabling decision has a legitimate role in countries eager to press ahead but rightly fearful of doing so without the opportunity of later calling a halt. It could also prove useful in those countries wishing to maintain the appearance of a healthy nuclear industry for a few more years, in the hope that something will turn up in the world outside to resolve their dilemma over power station choice.

Considerations such as these shaped our projections of installed nuclear capacity in Chapter 2. We did not attempt to incorporate them into a formal model of nuclear power development, but instead allowed them to interact with other influences and constraints to shape our judgement of the likely future of nuclear power in individual countries. Many of the new factors we have identified are subjective. This applies, for example, to the risk index, the accident surcharge, and the probability distributions of cost and performance parameters. We have provided a framework which we hope others will find useful in thinking about these problems, but until pressure groups and decision-makers in all countries

Table 10.1 *Whose views are challenged?*

Challenges nuclear proponent		Challenges nuclear opponent	
Accident experience	(Ch. 3)	Economics of an enabling	
Hidden costs of TMI	(Ch. 4)	decision	(Ch. 8)
The accident surcharge	(Ch. 5)		
The risk index	(Ch. 6)	Trade in nuclear electricity	(Ch. 9)
Economics of a nuclear			
programme	(Ch. 7)		

have debated these issues at length, no new mechanistic forecast of nuclear power growth will be any more accurate than its predecessors.

Table 10.1 divides the issues we have raised in this book according to whose entrenched views they most strongly challenge: the nuclear power proponent who would like the world to return to the uncomplicated pro-nuclear state presented at the beginning of Chapter 1, or the nuclear power opponent who believes reactors should not be built under any circumstances. The list of issues challenging nuclear proponents is longer, but this is not surprising, since the professional response of Chapter 1 appeared so convincing. The conclusions of Chapters 8 and 9 should also give nuclear opponents pause for thought; even if they successfully oppose a full-scale programme of nuclear reactors, there may be strong arguments for a limited nuclear programme or importing nuclear electricity.

Remaining open questions

While performing the work reported in this book we have frequently felt that every tentative answer we reached was accompanied by at least two new questions. In this final section we would like to share some of the more important of these questions with you; they require urgent investigation.

(i) If different views about the risks of nuclear power come largely from the different weights that people use when aggregating the risks of death, injury and anxiety, as we suggest in Chapter 6, then how do people decide which weights to use? What weights will they employ to combine risks with costs, environmental effects and so on? How might the weights and the scores of individual technologies be influenced by the actions of nuclear proponents and objectors? Will views converge with time as more experience is gained?

(ii) How will the accident surcharge of Chapter 5 vary with time? Extra experience will affect the probabilities assigned to class 1, 2 and 3 accidents, and will also increase the likelihood of an accident somewhere in the world. How do these two factors interact?

(iii) What happens to the net decision benefit of Chapter 8 if enabling decisions only give imperfect information about costs and performance? What benefit is gained if series ordering has to start before the first plant is completed? What happens if certain variables are correlated? How would our results be affected by decision-makers adopting risk-averse strategies? Do these refinements destroy the large positive benefits of the enabling decision?

(iv) Is there any way of resolving the dilemma whereby commitment to a major programme of nuclear construction appears not to be justified, and yet the only way to achieve *very* low capital costs is to embark on large-scale ordering of nuclear plant? Should the 1970s goal of having nuclear capital costs fall with each unit built be replaced by a more pragmatic endeavour to limit cost escalation?

(v) We discussed the pros and cons of trade in nuclear electricity in Chapter 9. What is the largest percentage of traded electricity that a country will accept? To what extent does it depend on the energy self-sufficiency of the country? How will the price of traded electricity be set? What will the price be?

These questions show that the future of nuclear power is by no means clearcut. At best we have been able to pinpoint some of the important issues and take the first steps towards resolving them. If we have helped any reader to think hard about the merits of different viewpoints we shall be satisfied. If that contemplation leads to an attack on one of the many unresolved questions we shall be pleased. If nuclear programmes develop exactly as we have projected we shall be amazed. One positive side-effect of the transition from nuclear optimism to scepticism is the realisation that all the glib answers are wrong.

Notes

1 Nuclear power certainties and doubts

1 'On thermodynamical grounds, which I can hardly summarize shortly, I do not much believe in the commercial possibility of induced radioactivity.' From a paper given by J. B. S. Haldane on 4 February 1923 and published as *Daedalus, or science and the future* (London, Kegan Paul, 1924).

2 Two substantial contributions were F. H. Schmidt and D. Bodansky, *The fight over nuclear power* (San Francisco, Albion, 1976), which concentrated on the USA, and G. Greenhalgh, *The necessity for nuclear power* (London, Graham and Trotman, 1980).

3 We cover the later periods in more detail, as excellent accounts of the early history of nuclear power already exist in D. Burn, *Nuclear power and the energy crisis* (London, Macmillan, 1978) and R. Williams, *The nuclear power decisions* (London, Croom Helm, 1980).

4 Although Williams (*Nuclear power decisions*) indicates on p. 30 that this event led indirectly to the establishment of the Nuclear Installations Inspectorate (NII).

5 Burn, *Nuclear power*, p. 15.

6 For a much fuller exposition, with the complete supporting arguments, see either of the books in note 2 above. Our intention here is to present the case briefly but fairly for the benefit of readers to whom it may be unfamiliar.

7 One UK Government study quantified the likely coal price increases as 50% by the year 2000 and 100% by 2025 above the late 1970s price level. The resulting nuclear cost advantage for electricity generation was forecast to be about 40% in 2000 and nearly 50% by 2025. *Energy technologies for the United Kingdom*, Vol. II, UK Department of Energy (London, HMSO, 1979), pp. 151, 158.

8 *Reactor safety study: An assessment of accident risks in US commercial nuclear power plants*, USA, Nuclear Regulatory Commission, WASH-1400 (1975).

9 As reported in Schmidt and Bodansky *Fight over nuclear power*, p. 78.

10 H. Inhaber, 'Risk of energy production', Atomic Energy Control Board of Canada, AECB-1119 (1978).

11 A view propounded most forcefully in F. Hoyle, *Energy or extinction* (London, Heinemann, 1977).

12 Fig. 1.1 is synthesised from high and low figures in three reports, all produced by the OECD Nuclear Energy Agency. These are: *Uranium: Resources, production and demand* (OECD/NEA and IAEA Paris, 1973 and Paris,

151

1975); and *Nuclear fuel cycle requirements and supply considerations through the long term* (OECD/NEA, Paris, 1978).

13 M. J. Prior, 'The economics of coal and nuclear power plants', IEA coal research (1978) was one of these.

14 Many independent studies have identified the real cost escalation of nuclear plants, particularly in the USA. These include: K. R. Shaw, *Energy Policy*, 7: 4 (1979), 321–8; R. N. Budwani, *Power Engineering*, 84: 5 (1980), 62–70; W. E. Mooz, *Energy*, 6: 3 (1981), 197–225; C. Komanoff, 'Power plant cost escalation', Komanoff Energy Associates (1981); J. H. Crowley and J. D. Griffith, *Nuclear Engineering International*, 27: 328 (1982), 25–8.

15 C. Komanoff, 'The Westinghouse PWR in the United States: Cost and performance history', *Issues in the Sizewell B Inquiry conference*, Vol. 2 (London, Polytechnic of the South Bank, 1982).

16 R. Hellman and C. J. C. Hellman, *The competitive economics of nuclear and coal power* (Lexington, Mass., D. C. Heath, 1983).

17 Reported in *Nuclear Engineering International*, 17: 328 (1982), 35.

18 The most comprehensive attack was contained in J. P. Holdren et al., 'Risk of renewable energy sources: A critique of the Inhaber report', Energy and Resources Group, University of California, mimeo (1979), a document somewhat longer than the subject of its critique.

2 Nuclear power in the Western world to 2000

1 OECD/NEA and IAEA, *Uranium: Resources, production and demand* (Paris, 1973).

2 OECD/NEA and IAEA, *Uranium: Resources, production and demand* (Paris, 1975).

3 OECD/NEA, *Nuclear fuel cycle requirements and supply considerations through the long term* (Paris, 1978).

4 International Nuclear Fuel Cycle Evaluation (INFCE), Working Group 1 final report (1979).

5 OECD/NEA, *Nuclear energy and its fuel cycle – prospects to 2025* (Paris, 1982).

6 An outline of the OECD/NEA methodology is provided in the introduction of the reference given in note 5 above.

7 IIASA, *Energy in a finite world: A global systems analysis*(1981), pp. 107–48.

8 The only countries likely to have significant fast reactor capacity (>1 GW) by the year 2000 are France, USSR and Japan. Three other countries, US, UK and FRG are considered to be possibilities for commercial FBR development.

9 The publications that were found to be generally useful and which were used in the compilation of a large number of the country profiles were: *Nuclear Engineering International*, published monthly; *Nuclear Europe*, published monthly; United Nations, *1980 Yearbook of world energy statistics* (UN, New York, 1981); OECD, *Energy balances of OECD countries 1971/81*, (Paris, 1983); G. Greenhalgh and E. Jeffs, *The nuclear industry almanac, 1983, Western Europe*, published by Nuclear Energy Intelligence, available from Alan Armstrong Associates, London (London, 1982); IEA/OECD, *Workshop on energy data of developing countries* (Paris, 1979).

10 In the UK, for example, Lord Bowden of Chesterfield is a vociferous supporter of the Candu, as revealed in a paper presented at a conference entitled 'Issues

in the Sizewell B Inquiry', held at the Polytechnic of the South Bank, London, 26–8 October 1982. (Proceedings published by the Polytechnic of the South Bank: *Issues in the Sizewell B Inquiry conference* (2 vols, London, 1982).

11 W. Walker and M. Lonnroth, *Nuclear power struggles: Industrial competition and proliferation control* (London, George Allen & Unwin, 1983), pp. 72–5.

12 Details of the AIF appraisal appear in *Nuclear Engineering International*, 28: 338 (1983), 10.

13 N. J. D. Lucas, *Energy in France: Planning, politics and policy* (London, Europa, 1979), pp. 195–207.

14 For an excellent account of the slow and often painful development of nuclear power in the UK see: R. Williams, *The nuclear power decisions: British policies 1953–1978* (London, Croom Helm, 1980).

15 The Monopolies and Mergers Commission *Central Electricity Generating Board: A report on the operation by the Board of its system for the generation and supply of electricity in bulk* (London, HMSO, 1981).

16 J. W. Jeffrey, *Energy Policy* 10: 2 (1982), 76–100.

17 CEGB, 'Sizewell B Power Station Public Inquiry: CEGB Statement of Case', Vol. I and Appendix D, April 1982.

18 C. D. Heising-Goodman, *Applied Energy*, 8 (1981), 19–49.

19 C. Everson, R. Eden, C. Hope, 'Argentina: The energy outlook', Cambridge Energy Research Group, Energy Discussion Paper 7, July 1981.

20 J. E. Katz and O. S. Marwah (eds), *Nuclear power in developing countries: An analysis of decision making* (Lexington, Mass., Lexington Books, 1982), pp. 79–96.

21 R. Eden and G. Jannuzzi, 'Brazil: The energy outlook', Cambridge Energy Research Group, Energy Discussion Paper 10, August 1981.

22 In several other countries reactors of a few hundred MW are in operation but represent the initial stages of nuclear development, with orders for the reactors generally being placed during the 1960s.

23 B. W. Ang, 'The structure of energy demand in East Asian developing countries', Ph.D. Thesis, University of Cambridge, October 1980.

24 R. Eden and C. Hope, 'Mexico: The energy outlook', Cambridge Energy Research Group, Energy Discussion Paper 19, April 1982.

25 Ang, 'East Asian developing countries'.

26 *Nuclear Engineering International*, 27: 322 (1982), 29–44.

27 Katz and Marwah, *Nuclear power in developing countries*, pp. 273–300.

28 Overseas Advisory Associates Inc., 'Towards a new pattern of energy and economic development for Taiwan, Republic of China', Detroit, Mich., February 1982.

3 The frequency of core meltdown accidents

1 Nuclear Energy Policy Study Group, *Nuclear power issues and choices* (Cambridge, Mass., Ballinger, 1977), p. 224.

2 The CEGB estimates that 1 in 40 meltdowns are likely to lead to a loss of containment. 'Reactor's safety network', *Guardian*, 24 February 1983, p. 4.

3 W. S. Humphrey and J. Stanislaw, *Energy Policy*, 7: 1 (1979), 29–42.

4 Commission on Energy and the Environment, *Coal and the Environment* (London, HMSO, 1981).

5 C. Bliss et al., 'Accidents and unscheduled events associated with non-nuclear energy resources and technology', MITRE corporation, for the Environmental Protection Agency (1979).

6 Where we have weighted each year equally to simplify the exposition. A more sophisticated analysis might weight each year proportionally to its output.

7 With a sample of n from an infinite population, $(\mu - \bar{x})/sn^{-\frac{1}{2}}$ has a student's t distribution with $n - 1$ degrees of freedom, where μ is the population mean, $\bar{x}$ the sample mean and s the sample standard deviation. Since the 97.5% point on the t_3 distribution is 3.1824, we can be 95% sure that μ is within $(3.1824 \times 0.09)/\sqrt{4} = 0.14$ of $\bar{x}$.

8 Deaths from Bliss et al. 'Accidents'; output from United Nations, *World energy supplies 1950–74* (New York, UN, 1976), p. 133, in million tonnes of coal equivalent.

9 P. S. Dasgupta and G. M. Heal, *Economic theory and exhaustible resources* (Welwyn Gdn City, Herts., Nisbet, 1979), p. 172.

10 United Nations, *World energy supplies 1950–74* (New York, UN, 1976), p. 707.

11 From L. R. Howles, 'Nuclear station achievement', *Nuclear Engineering International*, 26: 310 (1981), 43–5, plus 10% to account for centrally planned countries which are omitted from the *NEI* figures.

12 From L. R. Howles, 'Nuclear station achievement', *Nuclear Engineering International*, 27: 324 (1982), 14–16.

13 Data before 1975, from G. S. Lellouche, *Nuclear Technology*, 53 (1981), 231–4, excludes reactors with power levels less than 30 MW(e). Data since 1975, from 'Nuclear station achievement' in March or April issues of *Nuclear Engineering International*, excludes reactors smaller than 150 MW(e).

14 It is theoretically possible for a control rod fault at a shutdown reactor to lead to a local criticality incident which could, in turn, lead to a partial core meltdown.

15 *Nuclear Engineering International*, 27: 333 (1982), 30, presents the inconclusive results of the first quick look by camera inside the core of TMI-2 since the accident.

16 Subject to some technical conditions which ensure that it is meaningful to talk about an overall frequency of meltdowns per reactor year in LWR stations. These conditions include specifying that the frequency is constant through time, during the lifetime of each reactor and from reactor to reactor in the statistical sample that gives the operating experience to date.

17 If no core meltdowns have occurred in n reactor years of operation, and there is no other relevant source of information, the probability density function for the frequency of core meltdowns, θ per reactor year is given by $P_\theta = ne^{-n\theta}$. See also note 7 above.

18 Integrating the probability density function from note 17 shows that the probability that the frequency is less than any specified value θ is $1 - e^{-n\theta}$. Setting this equal to 0.95 gives $\theta_{0.95} = 3 \div n$, and inserting $n = 460$ reactor years gives the value of $\theta_{0.95}$ used in the text.

19 If one core meltdown has occurred in n reactor years of operation, the probability density function for the frequency of core meltdowns, θ, per reactor year is given by $P_\theta = n^2\theta e^{-n\theta}$. This is plotted in figure 3.2, with $n = 600$.

20 Integrating the probability density function from note 19 shows that the probability that the frequency is less than any specified value θ is

$1 - (1 + n\theta)e^{-n\theta}$. Setting this equal to 0.95 gives $\theta_{0.95} = 4.75 \div n$ and inserting $n = 600$ reactor years gives the value of $\theta_{0.95}$ used in the text.

21 Where the two values are $\theta_{0.05}$ and $\theta_{0.95}$ for one meltdown in 858 reactor years. Setting the expression in note 20 equal to 0.05 gives $\theta_{0.05} = 0.35 \div n$, and inserting $n = 858$ reactor years gives the value for $\theta_{0.05}$ used in the text.

22 Assuming 90% of the capacity in Chapter 2 is LWR, each reactor being 1.2 GW and operating at a lifetime load factor of 60%.

23 'Accident lessons incorporated into Sizewell's design claims CEGB', *Guardian*, 12 February 1983.

24 This brief summary cannot of course do justice to the complexity and subtlety of actual PRAs. WASH-1400 (note 25) and the Zion PRA (note 29) both run to several thousand pages. Readers are referred to these studies for further technical information.

25 Nuclear Regulatory Commission, *Reactor safety study: An assessment of accident risks in US commercial nuclear power plants*, WASH-1400 (1975).

26 H. W. Lewis et al., *Risk Assessment Review Group report to the US Nuclear Regulatory Commission*, NUREG CR-0400 (1978).

27 Nuclear Energy Policy Study Group, *Nuclear power issues and choices* (Cambridge, Mass., Ballinger, 1977), p. 229.

28 S. Levine and F. Stetson, *Nuclear Engineering International*, 27: 328 (1982), 35–8.

29 *Zion probabilistic safety study*, Commonwealth Edison Company, September 1981.

30 G. T. Klopp, *Power Engineering*, 8: 1 (1982), 51.

31 Inserting $\theta = 4.42 \times 10^{-5}$ per reactor year and $n = 858$ reactor years into the expression in note 20 gives the probability in the text.

32 'Recalculating the risks of nuclear accidents', *The Economist*, 31 July 1982, p. 77.

33 J. Gittus, 'On degraded core analysis', CEGB Proof of Evidence, P16, to Sizewell B Power Station Public Inquiry, p. 21.

34 B. Fischhoff et al., *Acceptable risk* (Cambridge University Press, 1982) p. 30.

35 J. P. Holdren, *Bulletin of the Atomic Scientists*, 32: 3 (1976), 20–2.

36 L. Phillips, 'The evaluation of risk estimates: Limitations to human judgement?', Brunel University Tutorial Paper 79–2 (1979), p. 36.

37 A CEGB witness at the Sizewell inquiry is quoted as saying that assessment work gave confidence 'that no major safety issue was outstanding and that, for aspects which had not been completely cleared, no major design changes or significant operational restrictions would be required'. *Guardian*, 12 February 1983.

38 As used for instance in G. Apostolakis and A. Mosleh, *Nuclear Science and Engineering*, 70 (1979), 135–49.

39 If two core meltdowns have occurred in n reactor years of operation, the probability density function for the frequency of core meltdowns, θ, per reactor year is given by $P(\theta)/P\theta = \frac{1}{2}n^3\theta^2 e^{-n\theta}$. Integrating this expression, the probability that the frequency is less than any specified value θ is $1 - [1 + n\theta + \frac{1}{2}(n\theta)^2]e^{-n\theta}$.

4 Hidden costs of the accident at Three Mile Island

1 K. R. Shaw, *Energy Policy*, 7: 4 (1979), 321–8.
2 R. N. Budwani, *Power Engineering*, 84: 5 (1980), 62–70.

3 J. G. Kemeny (Chairman), *Report of the President's Commission on the Accident at Three Mile Island*, New York, Pergamon Press (1979).
4 P. J. Taylor, 'The Windscale Fire, October 1957', Political Ecology Research Group Research Report RR-7, 34 Cowley Road, Oxford, England.
5 R. Masters, *Nuclear Engineering International*, 27: 323 (1982), 21–5.
6 *Nuclear Engineering International*, 28: 338 (1983), 9.
7 Various other costs might be attributed to the accident which will probably be of a lesser degree than those discussed (for example, a possible reduction in property values in the vicinity of the TMI site). Also, no attempt is made to quantify any possible benefits arising from the accident, such as subsequent improvements in operator training leading to a reduction in the likelihood of future reactor accidents.
8 L. R. Howles, 'Nuclear station achievement', *Nuclear Engineering International*, 23: 270 (1978), 25–8. These data appear quarterly thereafter.
9 This high *t* statistic reflects the fact that seasonal variability in 1980/81 was similar to that in 1978/79 (for example, the load factor for the January–March quarter was the highest in each period). However, the absolute levels of the four quarterly load factors in the second year after the accident were systematically lower than the corresponding figures for the year immediately prior to the accident.
10 International Atomic Energy Agency, 'Operating experience with nuclear power stations in member states in 1979', IAEA, Vienna (1981).
11 Budwani, *Power Engineering*, 84: 5 (1980), 62–70.
12 M. L. Baughman, P. L. Joskow and D. P. Kamat, *Electric Power in the United States: Models and Policy Analysis* (Cambridge, Mass., The MIT Press, 1979).
13 IEA/OECD, 'Energy Statistics 1974/1978', OECD, 2 rue André-Pascal, 75775 PARIS CEDEX 16, France.

5 Costs of nuclear accidents

1 Concern regarding the knock-on effects of reactor accidents does not date from the time of TMI but had been discussed, in qualitative terms, somewhat earlier. For example, Harvey Brookes writing in 'The economic and social costs of coal and nuclear electric generation', published by the Stanford Research Institute in 1976, made the following observation:

'The largest social costs of nuclear power may be associated with the political reactions to an accident or sabotage incident . . . Because of the greater sensitivity of the public to catastrophic accidents in comparison with statistical deaths, one should compute the possible costs of a shutdown or partial shutdown of all existing nuclear reactors for a long period of time following an accident to one reactor.'

This is also quoted in David L. Sills et al., *Accident at Three Mile Island: The human dimensions* (Boulder, Colorado, Westview Press, 1982).
2 If the comparison were to be broadened to include other options such as coal firing, then analogous surcharges should be added to their costs also; for example, to allow for the possibility that an unexpectedly severe greenhouse effect would force the closedown of coal stations before their planned date of retirement. We do not attempt such a calculation here.
3 Even this statement requires an assumption of risk neutrality. In the presence of significant risk aversion it would be necessary to work with the disutility of

consequences rather than the consequences themselves. We assume risk neutrality throughout.

4 Estimates of the maximum dose received by individual members of the public following the TMI accident fall in the range 40–70 millirem (400–700 μSv).

5 This figure is comparable to the data on operating experience in Chapter 3, but also includes reactors other than LWRs.

6 A complete analysis of experience to date, which assumes that the future will be the same as past experience, would allow that the frequency could be even higher (see Chapter 3).

7 The reverse argument could also be made – as the number of nuclear stations grows, safety standards will fall as complacency sets in and high-quality plant operators become difficult to find.

8 Current estimates of nuclear capital costs would put the figure nearer to $2 billion but the figure of $1 billion adopted here assumes a scrap or re-use value of certain station components.

9 This takes account of the fact that an accident can take place at any time during the lifetime of a reactor and will not necessarily occur at the start of its life as happened at TMI-2.

10 Department of Energy, Energy Paper Number 39, 'Energy Technologies for the United Kingdom', Vol. II Annexes (1979), Fig. C23, p. 158.

11 Note that the assumed capacity figures of 58% PWRs and 2% AGRs become 57% PWRs and 4% AGRs when expressed in terms of the number of reactors. This is because we assume that all future PWR reactors will be of 1200 MW capacity while future AGRs will remain at 600 MW.

12 CEGB, 'Sizewell B Power Station Public Inquiry – CEGB Statement of Case', Vol. 2, April 1982, pp. 82–3.

13 However, in the days immediately after the TMI accident, serious consideration was given to an evacuation of the local population and, in a situation characterised by much confusion, a recommendation was issued, on 30 March 1979, that pregnant women and pre-school age children within five miles of the plant leave the area temporarily.

14 It is easy to imagine cases where public opinion, expressed directly or through the political process could force the UK utilities into making one of the two strong responses following a class 2 accident.

15 For instance, if a 1 GW reactor closes midway through its planned 30-year operating lifetime, the extra cost is 0.6×316 million $\times 15 \times 0.33 = \$942$ million where the four factors are (i) the load factor, giving the number of GWyr of replacement generation required every year; (ii) the cost of 1 GWyr of alternative generation at 35 mills per kWh; (iii) the 15 years of replacement generation required and (iv) the discount factor at 5% per year to translate the annual payments to the date of commissioning.

16 For instance, the probability of the accident occurring between the tenth and twentieth year of operation is 24%. This is taken as the probability of the accident occurring close to the fifteenth year of operation.

17 The probabilities of closure are $0.025 + 0.57 \times 0.05 = 0.054$ for PWR, $0.025 + 0.04 \times 0.05 = 0.027$ for AGR. The probabilities of a drop in load factor are $0.57 \times 0.925 = 0.527$ for PWR, $0.04 \times 0.925 = 0.037$ for AGR.

18 CEGB, 'Sizewell B Power Station Public Inquiry – CEGB Statement of Case', Vol. 2, April 1982, pp. 82–3.

19 Ibid.

20 This type of argument is even stronger when applied to a country such as France where nuclear power is growing rapidly and provided 39% of electricity production in 1982.

21 *Nuclear Engineering International*, 27: 324 (1982), 10.

22 Alan Cottrell, *How Safe is Nuclear Energy?* (London, Heinemann, 1982). ch. 9.

23 John H. Crowley and Jerry D. Griffith, 'US construction cost rise threatens nuclear option', *Nuclear Engineering International*, 27: 328 (1982), 25–8.

24 The conclusion that it is the indirect effects of accidents, in which few lives may be lost, that may contribute the most important components of costs incurred, has been suggested elsewhere. See: P. Slovic, B. Fischhoff and S. Lichtenstein, 'Setting acceptable risk criteria and decision making', *Transactions of the American Nuclear Society*, 35 (1980), 400–1.

25 B. Fischhoff et al., 'How safe is safe enough? A psychometric study of attitudes towards technological risks and benefits', *Policy Sciences*, 8 (1978), 127–52.

6 Defining the risks of nuclear power

1 Theoretically, the risk imposers and risk receivers could reach agreement by a series of bargains and side payments to allow some level of risk to continue. However a whole suite of unrealistic conditions (such as full knowledge on both sides, no tactical behaviour inside each group and a well-defined outcome in default of agreement) are required for the agreed outcome to be optimal.

2 If the standards are more stringent than those which the risk imposers would anyway have chosen, which they must be if they are to have any effect.

3 See, for example, P. Burrows, *The economic theory of pollution control* (Oxford, Martin Robertson, 1979) for a fuller description of the economic approach.

4 B. L. Cohen, *Health Physics*, 38 (1980), 33–51.

5 See, for instance, 'Accident lessons incorporated into Sizewell's design claims CEGB', *Guardian*, 12 February 1983. There is some evidence that the NII might not be prepared to license even this design until further changes are made.

6 'Assessing US attitudes to numerical safety goals', *Nuclear Engineering International*, 27: 333 (1982), 15–16.

7 It has been dubbed the 'phlogiston theory of risk' by S. R. Watson, *Journal of the Society for Radiological Protection*, 1: 4 (1981), 21–5.

8 Or 'Deaths per some other unit of output'. Indeed we have done it ourselves in Chapter 1 and earlier in this chapter, and you probably did not think it at all odd.

9 As suggested for example in J. Reissland and V. Harries in 'A scale for measuring risks', *New Scientist*, 83 (1979), 809–11.

10 This being the technical expression for the illnesses and injuries that do not lead to death.

11 C. Starr, 'Social benefit versus technological risk', *Science*, 165 (1969), 1232–8.

12 B. Fischhoff et al., 'How safe is safe enough?', *Policy Sciences*, 8 (1978), 127–52.

13 What the end-points of the unknown and dread scales mean will be dealt with

later in the chapter, when we go one stage further and construct a numerical index of risk. For now, it is only necessary to accept that a higher score on these two scales means that a technology is more unknown or dread, i.e. more risky all other things equal.

14 And somehow weigh risk against other dimensions such as costs and environmental impacts. This is dealt with later.

15 Such as miscounting the drop in worker deaths going from technology II to I as 1.5 per GWyr, instead of 2.5.

16 Such as preferring the risk vector of II to that of I and the risk vector of some other technology III to II but then discovering a preference for the risk vector of I to that of III.

17 Mathematically

$$R_i = \sum_{j=1}^{n} w_j y_{ij}$$

where R_i = risk index of technology i
   n = number of attributes included in index (5 in our case). Attribute is the technical term for what we have previously called a dimension, or element
   y_{ij} = expected value of score of technology i on attribute j
   w_j = weight attached to attribute j.

18 See for example Department of Energy, *Energy technologies for the United Kingdom*, Vols. I and II: Energy Paper 39 (London, HMSO, 1979).

19 P. Slovic, B. Fischhoff and S. Lichtenstein, 'Characterizing perceived risk', in R. W. Kates and C. Hohenemser (eds), *Technological hazard managment* (Oelgeschlager, Gunn and Hain, 1982).

20 These include G. B. Baecher, M. E. Pate and R. de Neufville, 'Risk of dam failure in benefit-cost analysis', *Water Resources Research*, 16 (1980), 449–56; A. Birkhofer, 'The German risk study of nuclear power plants', *IAEA Bulletin*, 22: 5/6 (1980), 22–33; C. Bliss, P. Clifford, G. Goldgraben, E. Graf-Webster, K. Krickenberger, H. Maher and N. Zimmerman, *Accidents and unscheduled events associated with non-nuclear energy resources and technology* (Washington, D.C., MITRE Corporation for Environmental Protection Agency, 1979); R. J. Budnitz and J. P. Holdren, 'Social and environmental costs of energy systems', *Annual Review of Energy*, 1 (1976), 553–80; C. L. Comar and L. A. Sagan 'Health effects of energy production and conversion', *Annual Review of Energy*, 1 (1976), 581–660; J. H. Dunster 'The approach of a regulatory authority to the concept of risk', *IAEA Bulletin*, 22: 5/6 (1980), 123–8; G. Greenhalgh, *The necessity for nuclear power* (London, Graham and Trotman, 1980); L. D. Hamilton, 'Comparative risks from different energy systems: Evolution of the methods of studies', *IAEA Bulletin*, 22: 5/6 (1980), 35–71; D. Okrent, 'Comment on societal risk', *Science*, 208 (1980), 372–5; D. W. O. Rogers and R. J. Templin, 'Errors in a risk assessment of renewable resources, *Energy*, 5 (1980), 101–3.

21 H. Inhaber, 'Risk in hydroelectricity production', *Energy*, 3 (1978), 769–78, Rogers and Templin, 'Errors in a risk assessment'.

22 'It is not easy to weigh the benefits of reducing anxiety against those of saving life, but our society certainly does not require the saving of life to be given

complete priority over the reduction of anxiety.' J. H. Dunster, 'The approach of a regulatory authority to the concept of risk', *IAEA Bulletin*, 22: 5/6 (1980), 127.

23 This might go some way towards alleviating the worries of A. V. Cohen who perceptively notes 'There is a danger . . . that one man's set of utilities will be buried in submissions to decision makers and lost sight of.' R. F. Griffiths (ed) *Dealing with risk* (Manchester University Press, 1981), p. 32.

24 CEGB, private communication.

25 'U.S. nuclear experts reject "inadequate" Sizewell reactor', *Guardian*, 24 February 1983, p. 6.

7 The uncertain economics of a nuclear power programme

1 Charles Komanoff, 'The Westinghouse PWR in the United States: Cost and performance history', in *Issues in the Sizewell B Inquiry Conference*, Vol. 2 (London, Polytechnic of the South Bank, 1982).

2 A. Wilson, 'Construction time, cost and operating performance of PWR, AGR, and coal-fired generating plant', CEGB, 'Sizewell B Power Station Public Inquiry – CEGB Proof of Evidence', P8, November 1982, pp. 45–50.

3 An example from the physical sciences, having a close link with nuclear power because of its theoretical handling of data uncertainties in neutron transport calculations is D. E. Bartine, E. M. Oblow and F. R. Mynatt, *Nuclear Science and Engineering*, 55 (1974), 147.

4 Criticisms of the scope of sensitivity analyses performed by the CEGB came from The Monopolies and Mergers Commission, *Central Electricity Generating Board: A report on the operation by the Board of its system for the generation and supply of electricity in bulk* (London, HMSO, 1981).

5 In the UK, for example, oil-fired power stations, on which construction began in the early 1970s (and in one case as late as 1975), are coming on-line in the early 1980s, and facing the prospect of operating with lifetime load-factors around 20% instead of the 60–70% originally envisaged.

6 Richard Eden et al., *Energy economics – growth, resources and policies* (Cambridge University Press, 1981), pp. 75–6.

7 The importance of uncertainty in the energy field was a recurring theme at the 1982 IAEE/BIEE International Energy Conference held in Cambridge, UK. Key papers from this conference appear in: Paul Tempest (ed), *International energy markets* (London, Graham and Trotman, 1983).

8 P. Massé and R. Gibrat, 'Application of linear programming to investments in the electrical power industry', in J. R. Nelson (ed), *Marginal cost pricing in practice* (New Jersey, Prentice-Hall, 1964).

9 The general problem of linear programming was first developed and applied by George B. Dantzig and his co-workers in the US Department of the Air Force in 1947.

10 One of the first problems to which linear programming techniques were applied was that of the Berlin air-lift in 1948.

11 For a good account of the use of LP models for investment planning in the electricity sector see R. Turvey and D. Anderson, *Electricity economics: Essays and case-studies* (Baltimore, Md, Johns Hopkins University Press for the World Bank, 1977). For details of the LP model used in the work described in this chapter see Nigel Evans, 'Electricity supply modelling: Theory and case

study', Cambridge Energy Research Group, Energy Discussion Paper 14, September 1981.

12 CEGB, 'Sizewell B Power Station Public Inquiry – CEGB Statement of Case', Vol. 1, April 1982, p. 54.

13 The Sizewell decision itself is explored further in Chapter 8.

14 See note 2, Addendum 2, Tables 1 and 3.

15 In our central view, availabilities rise from a low level, during the early years of operation of a plant, to a plateau which is maintained for ten years, and then slowly decline as the plant ages. The plateau values are: coal 80%; AGR 75%; PWR 75%.

16 In Chapter 8 we provide details of a particular sampling scheme that enables us to draw statistically significant inferences from a relatively small number of computer runs.

8 The economics of enabling decisions

1 S. Ahmed and A. A. Husseiny, *Energy*, 3: 6 (1978), 669–700.

2 A. S. Manne and R. G. Richels, *Energy Policy*, 8: 1 (1980), 3–16.

3 A. S. Manne and R. G. Richels, *Energy*, 3: 6 (1978), 747–67.

4 Carolyn D. Heising, *Energy Policy*, 10: 2 (1982), 101–8.

5 C. W. Hope, 'Methods for assessing investment on research and development for renewable energy technologies', Ph.D. thesis, University of Cambridge, January 1980.

6 An excellent introduction to decision analysis is given in Howard Raiffa, *Decision analysis: Introductory lectures on choices under uncertainty* (Reading, Mass., Addison–Wesley, 1968).

7 If Sizewell B is rejected, either by the Inspector at the Public Inquiry, or by the government minister responsible, the probability of the CEGB immediately proposing the construction of a PWR at an alternative site, is extremely remote.

8 An indicator which is frequently used to choose between alternative projects is the net effective cost (NEC), much favoured by the CEGB. It is the annuitised net present cost for each project over its expected lifetime and includes fuel savings obtained by displacing plant with higher running costs. It takes no account of possible additional benefits arising from the establishment of a low-cost option, which may be built in increasing numbers in the future.

9 We use the term 'expected value' to represent the sum of all possible outcomes multiplied by their probability of occurrence i.e. expected value $= \sum_i P_i N_i$, where P_i is the probability of obtaining a value N_i for the NDB. Using this as our decision variable implies the government has a neutral attitude to risk, which can be supported by theoretical arguments for investments that are small compared to the wealth of the country.

10 For an early account of the use of this technique in the energy area see: M. D. McKay, W. J. Conover and D. E. Whiteman, Report LA-NUREG-6526-MS, Los Alamos Scientific Laboratory, New Mexico, August 1976.

11 See also ibid., for an account of this technique.

12 If $u_i, u_2, \ldots, u_n$ are independent uniform random variables and r_i is the rank of u_i, then $r_i - 1$ is the number of u_is less than u_i. For example, if $u_1 = 3.8$; $u_2 = 0.9$; $u_3 = 5.7$; then $r_1 = 2$; $r_2 = 1$; $r_3 = 3$.

13 A more detailed account of the theoretical background to the work described in this chapter appears in Nigel Evans, *Energy Economics*, 6: 1 (1984), 14–20.
14 The discount rate is also somewhat different from other uncertain variables in that its value in the future is covered by a small number of discrete possibilities (such as 5, 8 or 10%). The effect of changes in the discount rate can perhaps best be examined by performing a number of complete sensitivity studies, in each of which a different discount rate is chosen, and correlations between it and other variables are taken into account by making changes to the subjective probability intervals.
15 In Hope, 'Methods for assessing', the effect of varying the lifetimes of a large number of renewable energy technologies has been shown to be small.
16 Full details are provided in the reference cited in note 13.
17 A similar conclusion was reached in Chapter 7 where we showed that the probability of oil-fired plant proving economic for baseload generation is extremely low.
18 It is this variable which provides information on the relative proportion of baseload to peak electricity demand.
19 Council for the Protection of Rural England, *The economic case against Sizewell B* (CPRE, London, January 1983).
20 Steve Thomas, 'Worldwide nuclear plant performance revisited: An analysis of 1978–81', *Futures*, December 1982, pp. 517–32.
21 J. Von Neumann and O. Morgenstern, *Theory of games and economic behaviour* (Princeton University Press, NJ, 1947). Chapter 3 of this work discusses the concept of utility.

9 Trade in nuclear electricity

1 OECD/IAEA, *Uranium: Resources, production and demand*, (Paris, 1975).
2 The Organisation for Economic Co-Operation and Development (OECD) represents the countries of the developed world and consists of the countries of Western Europe, North America and Japan, Australia and New Zealand.
3 This simple representation is only appropriate provided conditions similar to those required to create an additive risk index in Chapter 6, and described in detail there, are satisfied. It also requires the population of the country to have a neutral attitude to uncertainty over the appropriate ranges of financial effects and risks.
4 Note that if we set the weight given to risks to zero in both countries, the condition for trade to occur reduces exactly to the traditional cost advantage condition, $CN_H + CT_H < CC_{WH}$ (or CN_{WH} if this is lower).
5 The view on risks from coal-fired power stations that we use in this chapter might, for example, include figures on public deaths similar to those produced by: R. A. D. Ferguson, *Comparative risks of electricity generating fuel systems in the UK* (Stevenage, Herts., Peter Peregrinus, 1981). This would reduce our coal public death score from a value of 80, used in Chapter 6, to below 10, sufficient to give a value of 40 for RC_{WH}, the figure used in the text.
6 Unipede group, 'Study of methods of calculating the costs of electricity generation', summarised in *Nuclear Engineering International*, 27: 329 (1982), 9.
7 At a 5% discount rate and assuming that capital costs represent one half of

total generating costs for PWRs, as indicated by French data presented in *Nuclear Europe* 4 (April 1982), 26.

8 *New Scientist*, 93: 1290 (1982), 229–31. The NII has since indicated that further changes may be required before it is prepared to grant Sizewell B an operating licence.

9 It should be added that increasing electricity trade might give greater bargaining power to nuclear power workers in exporting countries. In the event of a dispute, strike action could put out the lights in neighbouring countries as well as at home.

10 The UCPTE group has eight members: Austria, Belgium, France, Federal Republic of Germany, Italy, Luxembourg, Netherlands, Switzerland, and four associate members: Spain, Portugal, Greece, Yugoslavia. The Nordel group comprises Denmark, Finland, Iceland, Norway and Sweden.

A selected bibliography

We list here some of the publications that we have found most useful or interesting. We have made no attempt to be exhaustive, and in particular have not tried to include the wealth of individual journal articles that have helped shape our views.

Background

General

Although the focus of this book is nuclear power, it is impossible to study any one aspect of the energy scene in isolation.

R. J. Eden et al. *Energy economics* (Cambridge University Press, 1981). An authoritative view of the world energy scene and its likely evolution into the next century.

Council for Science and Society. *Deciding about energy policy* (London, CSS, 1979). An attempt to look at the questions that are involved in deciding which energy plan to follow.

Nuclear Power

G. Greenhalgh. *The necessity for nuclear power* (London, Graham and Trotman, 1980). A strong and coherent argument for the use of nuclear power. Much of our Chapter 1 runs along similar lines.

W. Patterson. *Nuclear power* (Harmondsworth, Middx, Penguin, 1976). A book that reaches an anti-nuclear conclusion after prolonged rational discussion of the issues.

Royal Commission on Environmental Pollution. *Sixth report: Nuclear power and the environment* (London, HMSO, Cmnd 6618, 1976). An authoritative look at nuclear power in the UK. Often called simply 'the Flowers report' after its principal author.

Economics and Decision Making

General

R. L. Keeney and H. Raiffa. *Decisions with multiple objectives. Preferences and value trade-offs* (New York, Wiley, 1976). The seminal work for those trying to make decisions which have wide-ranging consequences. Highly technical in parts.

164

D. W. Pearce and C. A. Nash. *The social appraisal of projects: A text in cost-benefit analysis* (London, Macmillan, 1981). Explains the basis of this technique including the principle of discounting. Includes several examples.

H. Raiffa. *Decision analysis* (Reading, Mass., Addison–Wesley, 1968). The theory of decision-making under uncertainty, presented for the non-specialist reader, with worked examples.

S. Reutlinger. *Techniques for project appraisal under uncertainty*, World Bank Staff Occasional Paper, Number 10, published for the World Bank by The Johns Hopkins University Press (Baltimore, Md, 1970). This monograph describes techniques for incorporating uncertainty into project appraisal. Includes case studies.

Nuclear Power

D. Burn. *Nuclear power and the energy crisis: Politics and the atomic industry*, published by Macmillan for the Trade Policy Research Centre (London, 1978). A well-written and provocative book which critically examines crucial stages of nuclear power development in both the US and UK.

The Monopolies and Mergers Commission. *Central Electricity Generating Board: A report on the operation by the Board of its system for the generation and supply of electricity in bulk* (London, HMSO, 1981). An official critique of the planning methods used by the CEGB. Forms an enlightening case study in applied economics.

R. Turvey and D. Anderson. *Electricity economics: Essays and case studies*, published by The Johns Hopkins University Press for the World Bank (Baltimore, Md, 1977). A standard reference for all aspects of electricity supply economics.

R. Williams. *The nuclear power decisions: British policies 1953–1978* (London, Croom–Helm, 1980). Describes in detail how vital decisions concerning nuclear power in the UK have actually been reached. It provides a striking contrast with our analysis of Chapter 8.

Risks

General

P. Burrows. *The economic theory of pollution control* (Oxford, Martin Robertson, 1979). Explains in detail how economists would control threats to the environment.

B. Fischhoff et al. *Acceptable risk* (Cambridge University Press, 1981). Evaluates the different methods for deciding whether a risk is acceptable, placing emphasis on the wider social aspects.

J. Glover. *Causing death and saving lives* (Harmondsworth, Middx, Penguin, 1977). Philosophical views of the justification for threatening life, clearly and succinctly explained.

R. C. Schwing and W. A. Albers Jnr, (eds). *Societal risk assessment: How safe is safe enough?* (New York, Plenum Press, 1980). Contributions to the debate about risk assessment. Full of important ideas.

Nuclear Power

A. Cottrell. *How safe is nuclear energy?* (London, Heinemann, 1981). A short impartial guide, written for the layman, by one of the UK's leading authorities on nuclear power.

H. Inhaber. *Energy risk assessment* (New York, Gordon and Breach Science, 1982). Presents a method for calculating the total risks from energy sources.

Created a bitter controversy which is commendably recognised by including critics' reactions as an appendix.

J. G. Kemeny (Chairman). *Report of the President's Commission on the Accident at Three Mile Island* (New York, Pergamon, 1979). The official report on the worst nuclear accident to date, and a model for how the results of an inquiry should be published.

Statistics

Any one of a large number of books provides the statistical background necessary to follow the detailed arguments in several chapters. For example,

C. Chatfield. *Statistics for technology* (London, Chapman and Hall, 1970).

Journals

And finally two journals that are essential reading for anyone wanting to keep abreast of nuclear policy issues.

Energy Policy, published quarterly by Butterworths, has articles on all aspects of energy planning.

Nuclear Engineering International, published monthly by Business Press International Ltd, concentrates on the latest nuclear power developments.

Index